Tanzania:

Malaria Operational Plan FY 2014

TABLE OF CONTENTS

ABBREVIATIONS AND ACRONYMS

ACT	Artemisinin-based combination therapy
ADDO	Accredited Drug Dispensing Outlet
AL	Artemether-lumefantrine
AMFm	Affordable Medicines Facility-malaria
ANC	Antenatal care
BCC	Behavior change communication
CCA	Community change agent
CCHP	Comprehensive Council Health Plans
CDC	U.S. Centers for Disease Control & Prevention
CHW	Community health workers
CMS	Central Medical Store
COMMIT	Communication and Malaria Initiative in Tanzania
DFID	Department for International Development (U.K.)
DHMT	District Health Management Team
DHS	Demographic & Health Survey
FANC	Focused antenatal care
FELTP	Field Epidemiology and Laboratory Training Program
FSN	Foreign service national
FY	Fiscal year
Global Fund	Global Fund to Fight AIDS, Tuberculosis & Malaria
GoT	Government of Tanzania
HIS	Health information system
HIV	Human Immunodeficiency Virus
HMIS	Health management information system
IHI	Ifakara Health Institute
IMCI	Integrated management of childhood illness
IPTp	Intermittent preventive treatment in pregnancy
IRS	Indoor residual spraying
ITN	Insecticide-treated mosquito net
JSI	John Snow, Inc.
LGA	Local Government Authority
LLIN	Long-lasting insecticide-treated net
M&E	Monitoring and evaluation
MEEDS	Malaria Early Epidemic Detection System
MIP	Malaria in pregnancy
MIS	Malaria Indicator Survey
MOHSW	Ministry of Health & Social Welfare
MOP	Malaria Operational Plan
MSD	Medical Stores Department
NATNETS	National Insecticide-Treated Nets Program
NBS	National Bureau of Statistics
NGO	Non-governmental organization
NIMR	National Institute for Medical Research
NMAC	National Malaria Advisory Committee
NMCP	National Malaria Control Program
NPO	National Program Officer

PEPFAR	President's Emergency Plan for AIDS Relief
RBM	Roll Back Malaria
RDT	Rapid diagnostic test
RHMT	Regional Health Management Team
RTI	Research Triangle Institute
SMC	Safe Motherhood Campaign
SP	Sulfadoxine-pyrimethamine
SPA	Service Provision Assessment
TDY	Temporary duty
THMIS	Tanzania HIV & Malaria Indicator Survey
TNVS	Tanzania National Voucher Scheme
U5CC	Under-five catch-up campaign
UCC	Universal coverage campaign
UNHCR	United Nations Refugee Agency
UNICEF	United Nations Children's Fund
USAID	United States Agency for International Development
USG	United States Government
WHO	World Health Organization
WHOPES	World Health Organization Pesticide Evaluation Scheme
WRAIR	Walter Reed Army Institute of Research
ZRC	Zonal Resource Center
ZMCP	Zanzibar Malaria Control Program

EXECUTIVE SUMMARY

Malaria prevention and control are major foreign assistance objectives of the U.S. Government (USG). In May 2009, President Barack Obama announced the Global Health Initiative (GHI), a comprehensive effort to reduce the burden of disease and promote healthy communities and families around the world. Through the GHI, the United States will help partner countries improve health outcomes, with a particular focus on improving the health of women, newborns, and children.

The President's Malaria Initiative (PMI) is a core component of the GHI, along with HIV/AIDS and tuberculosis. PMI was launched in June 2005 as a five-year, $1.2 billion initiative to rapidly scale up malaria prevention and treatment interventions and reduce malaria-related mortality by 50% in 15 high-burden countries in sub-Saharan Africa. With passage of the 2008 Lantos-Hyde Act, funding for PMI was extended and, as part of the GHI, the goal of PMI was adjusted to reduce malaria-related mortality by 70% in the original 15 countries by the end of 2015. Programming of PMI activities follows the core principles of GHI: encouraging country ownership and investing in country-led plans and health systems; increasing impact and efficiency through strategic coordination and programmatic integration; strengthening and leveraging key partnerships, multilateral organizations, and private contributions; implementing a woman- and girl-centered approach; improving monitoring and evaluation; and promoting research and innovation.

In June 2005, the United States Government (USG) selected the United Republic of Tanzania (including the Mainland and Zanzibar) as one of the first of three countries to be included in PMI. Malaria is a major public health problem in Tanzania. Although dramatic progress in malaria control has been made in recent years with the scale up of malaria prevention and treatment interventions, nearly all 42 million residents on the Mainland and all 1.3 million persons in Zanzibar are still at risk of infection.

The most recent national-level data for malaria interventions in Tanzania comes from the 2011-12 Tanzania HIV/AIDS-Malaria Indicator Survey (THMIS) and shows further impressive improvements in nearly all malaria indicators when compared with 2005 and 2008-09 figures. Ninety-one percent of Mainland households owned at least one insecticide-treated mosquito net (ITN), with 72% of children under five and 75% of pregnant women sleeping under an ITN. This compares with just 63% ownership and 64% and 57% usage in the 2008-09 DHS. In Zanzibar, ITN ownership and usage fell somewhat when compared with the 2008-08 DHS; 74% of households now own at least one ITN and estimates of use among children under five and pregnant women are 51% and 36%, respectively. Malaria prevalence in Zanzibar remained extremely low at less than 1% in the 2011-12 THMIS.

Within the United Republic of Tanzania, the National Malaria Control Program (NMCP) on the Mainland and the Zanzibar Malaria Control Program (ZMCP) have independent malaria control programs. The Mainland has multiple active grants from the Global Fund to Fight AIDS, Tuberculosis and Malaria (Global Fund), including Rounds 1, 7, 8, and 9. These grants have provided most of the funding for the universal ITN campaign and for scale up of artemisinin-based combination therapies (ACTs), and a nationwide pilot of the distribution of subsidized ACTs in the private sector (the Affordable Medicines Facility-Malaria, or AMFm), which ended in late 2012. The British Department for International Development (DFID) is also providing $27 million in malaria funding from 2013-2018.

This PMI FY 2014 Malaria Operational Plan was developed with the NMCP on the Mainland and the ZMCP and in collaboration with other malaria control partners. The proposed activities have been reviewed and approved by both malaria control programs. The proposed FY 2014 budget for the country is $45 million. The major activities to be supported by PMI include the following:

Insecticide-treated Nets (ITNs): A total of 18.2 million free long-lasting ITNs were distributed during the Mainland's universal coverage campaign between September 2010 and October 2011. Most of the ITNs were procured by Global Fund; PMI support included logistics management and training of the community volunteers who distributed the ITNs within their villages and carried out follow-up visits to ensure that the nets were appropriately hung and used. As a means of sustaining universal coverage, PMI also supported the procurement and distribution of more than 900,000 ITNs through the Tanzania National Voucher Scheme that allows pregnant women and caregivers of infants to obtain highly-subsidized ITNs through local retail stores. A 2011/12 nationwide health survey showed that >90% of all households had one or more ITNs. In Zanzibar, between January and March 2012, a universal coverage campaign distributed more than 660,000 free ITNs throughout the islands.

Since the voucher system provides only about one-half of the 1.3 million ITNs needed each year to cover all newborns, distribution through school-based campaigns is being piloted as an additional way to maintain high net coverage rates. PMI procured 510,400 ITNs for the pilot school-based ITN distribution in three regions in southern Tanzania.

With FY 2014 funding, PMI will procure 1.2 million ITNs for the ITN keep-up program. On Zanzibar, where universal coverage with ITNs has been achieved, the Global Fund will procure the 230,000 ITNs required for continuous distribution through antenatal clinics to sustain high coverage rates; PMI funds will not be needed These commodity procurements will be accompanied with behavior change and communication (BCC) activities to promote demand for and correct usage of the nets.

Indoor Residual Spraying (IRS): In late 2012 and early 2013, PMI supported targeted spraying of 665,024 structures (with 95% coverage) in all 18 districts of Kagera, Mwanza, and Mara Regions of Lake Zone on the Mainland, protecting about 3.5 million people. Because of increasing insecticide resistance, carbamate insecticides were used in Kagera Region and three districts of Mwanza Region, where resistance to pyrethroids has been detected; the remaining districts were sprayed with pyrethroids. To date, Zanzibar has received seven rounds of IRS. During 2012, targeted and focal spraying with two rounds of a carbamate insecticide covered 267, 680 structures on the islands and protected about 1.3 million residents in districts that had reported more than 2 malaria cases/1,000 population.

.

With FY 2014 funding on the Mainland, PMI will support one round of IRS with Actellic CS in the targeted areas of Mwanza and Mara, and expand IRS using Vectron to the Ngeita and Kigoma regions which currently have the highest malaria prevalence in Tanzania. In total, 849,450 structures will be sprayed, protecting approximately 4.7 million people. Spraying in the Ngeita region will be done as part of a public-private partnership with Geita Gold Mine, which will contribute approximately $200,000 towards the operational costs of the spraying. Spraying will be suspended in Kagera region where all districts have had at least five rounds of spraying, and close entomologic and epidemiologic monitoring will be carried out. In Zanzibar, PMI will support only focal spraying with one round of Actellic CS in villages reporting more than 2 confirmed cases/1,000 population. Approximately 20,000 structures will be sprayed, protecting 101,800 people.

Malaria in Pregnancy (MIP): WHO recommends control and prevention of MIP via a three-pronged approach: distribution of ITNs through antenatal care clinics, provision of intermittent preventive treatment of pregnant women with SP (IPTp), and prompt case management of pregnant women with malaria. Both the Mainland and Zanzibar implement all three activities, however due to low prevalence in Zanzibar, the ZMCP is revising their policy and considering the discontinuation of IPTp.

Although antenatal clinic (ANC) attendance is almost universal (96% of pregnant women make at least one visit), IPTp coverage with two doses of sulfadoxine-pyrimethamine (SP) have remained stagnant at about 25% to 30% for the past five years. To promote increased coverage of interventions delivered through the ANC, Tanzania revived its Malaria in Pregnancy Task Force, a group including staff from the NMCP and Reproductive Health Unit of the Ministry of Health, together with other relevant stakeholders. This group has proposed changes to Tanzania's policy on IPTp in line with new WHO recommendations for a dose of SP for IPTp at each antenatal clinic visit beginning in the second trimester of pregnancy. PMI staff and PMI-supported implementing partners continue to play an active role in promoting this change. On Zanzibar, the 2011-12 DHS showed that the proportion of pregnant women completing the recommended two doses of IPTp remains at just 48% in spite of concerted efforts to improve these rates. With the low prevalence of malaria on the islands, PMI and ZMCP carried out a study that showed that only 0.8% of pregnant women had malaria parasitemia at the time of delivery. Based on these data, Zanzibar is considering shifting from IPTp to intermittent screening of pregnant women for malaria and treatment of those who are found to be infected.

With FY 2014 funds, PMI will continue to support promotion of the new IPTp policy, development of national training materials for that policy, and nationwide rollout of the new guidelines. Efforts will continue to ensure that ANC clients are counseled on the importance of IPTp through investments in the Safe Motherhood Campaign and to provide for more consistent supplies of SP for IPTp at ANC clinics. The commodities partner will strengthen national and zonal commodity forecasting and distribution as well as facility-based requisitions and reporting. In Zanzibar, PMI will support the intermittent screen and treat policy for a limited period to time before a transition can be made to passive case detection of malaria in pregnancy.

Case Management: In 2012, the NMCP changed its policy to require that all suspected cases of malaria be confirmed by laboratory test prior to treatment; Zanzibar had already changed its policy earlier. With FY 2013 funding, PMI is procuring about 4 million rapid diagnostic tests (RDTs) for Mainland; Zanzibar's needs for RDTs are already covered by the Global Fund. PMI continues to support training in microscopy and development and implementation of a quality assurance/quality control program for both malaria microscopy and RDTs on the Mainland and Zanzibar. During the past 12 months, PMI procured about 6 million ACT treatments to avoid stockouts in public health facilities on the Mainland; all ACT needs for Zanzibar were met by the Global Fund. PMI also supported updating the curricula of training institutions on malaria diagnostics and treatment, as well as refresher training of District Malaria Focal Persons and District Health Management Team staff. PMI continued to provide technical assistance for quantification of annual RDT and ACT needs and procurement planning. PMI also contributed to an integrated health service delivery project in Lake Zone with co-funding from the USAID Maternal and Child Health and HIV/AIDS programs.

With FY 2014 funding, PMI plans to procure up to 400,000 RDTs for Zanzibar and up to 1.2 million RDTs for the Mainland, but the final quantities procured will depend on Global Fund disbursements, as most of the needs may be covered by Global Fund. PMI will continue roll out of the quality assurance/quality control system for both microscopy and RDTs on the Mainland and Zanzibar. PMI will procure approximately 3 million ACT treatments for the public sector on the Mainland or for emergency use if stockouts are imminent. PMI will continue to provide technical assistance for quantification of annual RDT and ACT needs and support the integrated commodity logistics system to ensure availability of ACTs and other commodities in health facilities. To confirm the continued efficacy of the first-line antimalarial drug in Tanzania, PMI will support antimalarial drug efficacy testing on the Mainland. PMI will also procure about 50,000 RDTs and the same number of ACT treatments for UNHCR refugee camps in western Tanzania, whose populations continue to decline.

Epidemic Surveillance and Response: During the past year, PMI continued to support and strengthen the Malaria Early Epidemic Detection System (MEEDS) on Zanzibar to identify and respond to sudden increases in malaria transmission. Health facility-based early epidemic detection sites now exist in all 142 government health facilities in Zanzibar. This system has already detected several small outbreaks and investigations were launched. PMI efforts to help the Ministry of Health establish a similar surveillance network in Lake Zone near Lake Victoria have proceeded slower than expected due to problems launching the electronic reporting component of the system.

With FY 2014 funding, PMI will continue to support the paper-based malaria surveillance system in Lake Zone until an electronic system is up and running. On Zanzibar, PMI will continue to support the MEEDS in all 142 public health facilities and approximately 20 additional private facilities.

Monitoring and Evaluation (M&E): During the past year, PMI has continued its support to the NMCP's and ZMCP's strategic information system, which now includes information from a wide range of national and sub-national household surveys, the health management information system, and other more specific studies, and also provided funding for supervisory and quality assurance visits to health facilities. Entomology technicians have been trained and entomologic monitoring of mosquito abundance and insecticide resistance established at 14 sites on the Mainland and seven on the islands where PMI is supporting IRS.

With FY 2014 funding, PMI will continue support to the NMCP's and ZMCP's strategic information systems, together with funding for supervisory and quality assurance visits to health facilities and continued entomologic and insecticide resistance monitoring. Funding will also be provided for planning of the 2014-15 Demographic and Health Survey.

Behavior Change Communication (BCC): During the past year, PMI has supported BCC efforts on both the Mainland and Zanzibar disseminating messages related to the Malaria No More campaign and the Safe Motherhood campaign which delivers malaria and other health messages to pregnant women. The 2011/12 THMIS reported that 92% of women knew a symptom of malaria, and awareness of malaria is universal at over 98%. Eighty three percent of women and 91% of men had heard or seen the Malaria Haikubaliki (No More Malaria) slogan used on all malaria BCC in Tanzania, and 57% of women and 67% of men had heard or seen a malaria prevention message. The survey also found that women understand that pregnant women are at high risk of malaria (90%), that they could protect their children from malaria (82%), and that it was important to sleep under a net every night (93%).

With FY 2014 funding, PMI will continue to support implementation of the national strategy plan for BCC. Activities will include continued support for the Safe Motherhood campaign and messages focusing on the changing malaria situation in Zanzibar and in certain regions of the Mainland, such as the Lake Zone. Zanzibar BCC messages will focus on messages related to the continued risk of malaria despite reductions in prevalence and the need to be vigilant about malaria prevention and control activities. In the Kagera region, where IRS is being scaled-down, messages will focus on the rational and the importance of using other malaria prevention measures, such as ITNs.

Health Systems Strengthening and Integration: During the past year, PMI has worked to build capacity in the ministries of health and malaria control programs of Mainland and Zanzibar to strengthen their capacity for planning, implementing, and managing malaria control activities and to expand PMI's integration with other USG programs. To help deal with the severe shortage of health staff, PMI also contributes to a project to promote recruitment and retention of health workers. PMI contributed to the two-year Tanzanian Field Epidemiology and Laboratory Training Program (FELTP). Trainees from this program have participated in various malaria control activities at NMCP and ZMCP, including malaria surveillance and outbreak investigations and will return to the Ministry of Health on completion of their training. PMI is also working with the U.S. Department of Defense to train and certify laboratory technicians for improved performance of both microscopy and RDTs for malaria diagnosis.

With FY 2014 funding, PMI will help the NMCP and ZMCP to provide supportive supervision and improve coordination among malaria partners. PMI will continue to contribute, along with USAID HIV and other health funds, to health systems strengthening activities that include financing governance, and health workforce recruitment and retention. PMI will also continue to co-fund with PEPFAR the training of Tanzanian epidemiologists through the FELTP and will provide funding for improving laboratory diagnosis of malaria.

STRATEGY

1. INTRODUCTION

Malaria prevention and control is a major foreign assistance objective of the U.S. Government (USG). In May 2009, President Barack Obama announced the Global Health Initiative (GHI) to promote healthy communities and families around the world. Through the GHI, the United States will help partner countries improve health outcomes, with a particular focus on improving the health of women, newborns and children. The GHI is a global commitment to invest in healthy and productive lives, building upon and expanding the USG's successes in addressing specific diseases and issues in a sustainable fashion.

The President's Malaria Initiative (PMI) is a core component of the GHI, along with HIV/AIDS, and tuberculosis. PMI was launched in June 2005 as a five-year, $1.2 billion initiative to rapidly scale up malaria prevention and treatment interventions and reduce malaria-related mortality by 50% in 15 high-burden countries in sub-Saharan Africa. With passage of the 2008 Lantos-Hyde Act, funding for PMI was extended through FY 2014 and, as part of the GHI, the goal of PMI has been adjusted to reduce malaria-related mortality by 70% in the original 15 countries by the end of 2015. This will be achieved by reaching 85% coverage of the most vulnerable groups — children under five years of age and pregnant women — with proven preventive and therapeutic measures, including artemisinin-based combination therapies (ACTs), insecticide-treated nets (ITNs), intermittent preventive treatment of pregnant women (IPTp), and indoor residual spraying (IRS).

Through GHI and PMI, the USG is committed to working closely with host governments and within existing national malaria control plans. Efforts are coordinated with other national and international partners, including the Global Fund to Fight AIDS, Tuberculosis and Malaria (Global Fund), Roll Back Malaria (RBM), the World Bank Malaria Booster Program, and the non-governmental and private sectors, to ensure that investments are complementary and that RBM and Millennium Development Goals are achieved.

This document presents a detailed PMI implementation plan for FY 2014 in Tanzania. It briefly describes the current status of malaria control and prevention policies, planned interventions, challenges and unmet needs, and the planned FY 2014 PMI activities. The operational plan was developed in close consultation with the National Malaria Control Program (NMCP) and the Zanzibar Malaria Control Program (ZMCP) and with the participation of many national and international partners involved in malaria prevention and control in Tanzania. The total amount of PMI funding requested for Tanzania in FY 2014 is $45 million

1. MALARIA SITUATION IN TANZANIA

On the Mainland, 93% of the population lives in areas where malaria is transmitted, while the entire population of Zanzibar is prone to malaria infection. Unstable seasonal malaria transmission occurs in approximately 20% of the country, while stable malaria with seasonal variation occurs in another 20%. The remaining malaria endemic areas in Tanzania (60%) are characterized as stable perennial transmission. *Plasmodium falciparum* accounts for 96% of malaria infection in Tanzania, with the remaining 4% due to *P. malariae* and *P. ovale*.

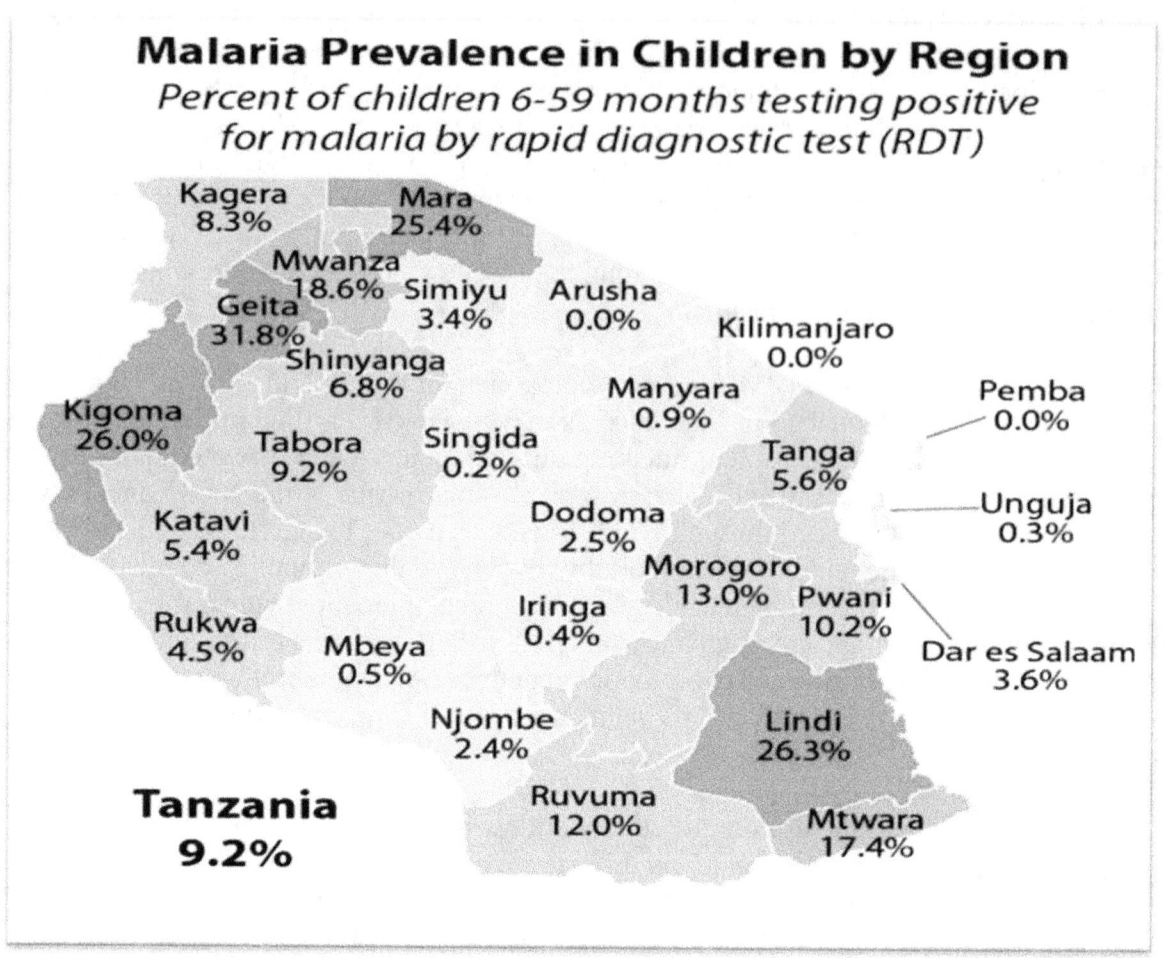

The principal vectors of malaria on the Mainland are the *Anopheles gambiae* complex (*An. gambiae s.s* and *An. arabiensis*). In Zanzibar, high coverage of ITNs and IRS have changed the composition of the malaria vector population. Routine entomological data show that *An. arabiensis*, which made up less than 4% of the population before scaling up of vector control interventions in 2005, represented almost 90% of the population in 2010, replacing the more efficient malaria vector, *An. Gambiae s.s.*

The 2011–2012 Tanzania HIV/AIDS Malaria Indicator Survey (THMIS) showed that 10% of Mainland children under five had tested positive for malaria, down from 18% in the 2008-2009 THMIS. Prevalence varied by region variation from <1% in the highlands of Arusha to 26% along the Lake Victoria shores (figure above). The same survey showed a much lower malaria prevalence of 0.2% in Zanzibar. On the Mainland, more than 40% of all outpatient attendances are attributable to malaria, resulting in an estimated 10-12 million clinical malaria cases annually. The NMCP estimates that 60,000-80,000 malaria deaths occur annually in the Mainland among all age groups.

Tanzania registered a 45% reduction in all cause under-five mortality from 146/1000 live births in 1999 to the current level of 81/1000 live births in 2010.

Infant and Under-five Mortality Rates for Five-year Periods Preceding Nationwide Household Surveys, Tanzania				
	1999 DHS	2004-05 DHS	2007-08 THMIS	2009-10 DHS
Infant mortality rate (95% C.I.)	99.1 (85-113)	68.0 (61-75)	57.7 (50-65)	51 (44-57)
Under-five mortality rate (95% C.I.)	146.6 (128-165)	112.0 (103-122)	91.4 (83-100)	81 (72-90)

The trend analysis of 1999 -2012 demographic surveys shows that the decline was greater in rural areas compared to urban areas, and more in medium to high malaria risk areas, indicating that interventions are reaching the poor and the more at risk populations. (January 2012 Roll Back Malaria report of *Progress and Impact series: Focus on Mainland Tanzania*)

2. MALARIA CONTROL PROGRAMS

Two separate Ministries of Health operate in the United Republic of Tanzania, one for the Mainland and one for Zanzibar. Each Ministry has its own malaria control program and malaria strategic plan. The National Malaria Control Program (NMCP) serves only the Mainland, while the Zanzibar Malaria Control Program (ZMCP) serves Zanzibar.

Mainland
Under the leadership of a Program Manager, the NMCP is organized into five cells: case management; vector control; ITNs; information and education; and monitoring and evaluation (including operations research). Each cell consists of a Team Leader and two to four staff members. The ZMCP has similar organizational units and a comparable staff.

The Mainland's NMCP has established several committees to coordinate and direct national malaria control policies and priorities. The Malaria Control Steering Committee is the body that is expected to provide strategic and policy direction for malaria control on Mainland. It is supposed to be chaired by the Chief Medical Officer, but has never been put in place. The ITN strategies and policies are coordinated through the National Insecticide Treated Nets (NATNETS) Program. A diagnostics and case management working group guides NMCP policies/strategies for strengthening and expanding malaria case management. In early 2009, an M&E technical working group was formed. PMI is represented on each of these working groups.

The NMCP and ZMCP each have malaria strategic plans ending in 2013 and both malaria programs are currently developing their new strategic plans, with input from PMI and other partners, which will cover the time period for the FY 2014 MOP. While they have shared their visions for their new strategic plans, as of writing of this MOP, both the strategic plans were in draft form. Thus, several of the interventions proposed are based on draft plans and may change before implementation of this FY 2014 MOP.

The NMCP strategic plan for 2014-2020, which is under development, includes the following goals:

- To reduce malaria morbidity and malaria deaths by 80% from the 2011 levels by 2020.
- To reduce malaria prevalence from 10% in 2012 to 1% in 2020.
- To reach the pre-elimination phase of malaria by 2020, defined as 1 case per thousand population.

To implement the new strategic plan the NMCP will address the thematic areas of 1) malaria case management, 2) integrated malaria vector control, 3) supportive interventions, such as behavior change communication (BCC) and monitoring and evaluation (M&E), and 4) program management. Each thematic area has objectives and strategies that support the overarching program goals.

Malaria Case Management
The principal objectives of malaria case management are to reduce vulnerability to malaria infections and morbidity/mortality among vulnerable populations and to ensure that all people with malaria have access to appropriate, timely treatment.

Integrated Malaria Vector Control
The objectives of integrated vector control are: 1) to achieve and maintain universal access of ITNs in order to have at least 80% appropriate use by 2020, 2) to consolidate the scope of IRS intervention to protect at least 85% of the population living in areas selected using evidence-based criteria, 3) to scale-up larviciding interventions by 2020 to selected (urban) areas where breeding sites are few, fixed, and findable, and 4) to promote effective environmental management for malaria control among at least 80% of communities through local government authorities in all districts.

Supportive interventions
The main objectives are: 1) improve BCC so that by 2020, 80% of all population at risk of malaria will be aware of the appropriate use of malaria prevention and treatment interventions, 2) to attain 100% reporting of routine and periodic key malaria indicators from all districts, 3) to strengthen malaria surveillance to detect 100% of malaria epidemics within one week of onset, 4) to effectively manage malaria epidemics within two weeks of detection, and 5) to strengthen monitoring and evaluation of malaria control interventions, activities, policies and strategies.

Program Management
The principal objective is to strengthen capacity in program management, resource mobilization and coordination at all levels.

Zanzibar
The ZMCP's 2013-2018 Strategic Plan focuses on pre-elimination. The vision of the ZMCP is that by 2018 Zanzibar will have no locally-acquired malaria cases. The ZMCP expects to achieve this by providing quality, affordable, and cost effective anti-malarial interventions to all people

14

in Zanzibar and by maintaining and expanding a well-performing epidemic detection and response system. The operational objectives in the ZMCP Strategic Plan are:

- To test 100% of suspected malaria cases with a parasitological test and provide radical treatment to 100% of confirmed cases by 2015.
- To achieve and maintain 100% coverage with prevention measures in all targeted areas
- To conduct active case detection in all eligible *shehias* (hamlets) by 2015.
- To increase the percentage of febrile cases reporting to health facilities within 24 hours of onset of illness to 80% by 2017.
- To establish functional coordination structures for malaria elimination at national, district and *shehia* levels by 2013.

3. INTEGRATION, COLLABORATION, AND COORDINATION

Funding and Integration with Key Development Partners
The 2010 National Health Accounts showed that in 2010, donor expenditure on malaria control increased from 18% in 2005/2006 to 40% in 2009/2010, while Government of Tanzania funding decreased from 22% to 19% over the same period.[1] The Global Fund and PMI provide more than 90% of funding to Tanzania Mainland and Zanzibar malaria control programs. Ninety nine percent of the total malaria control budget in Zanzibar comes from external resources.[2] This does not take into account staff salaries, which are paid by the government. PMI is the largest donor to the ZMCP, followed by the Global Fund. Other donors include WHO, UNICEF, and African Development Bank, JICA, Danida, DFID, and the research institutions.

The Global Fund lifetime approved budget for malaria control in Tanzania mainland is $360.4 million, out of which $331 million (81.9%) is already disbursed through rounds 1,4,7,8,9, and single stream funding. The approved next five-year single stream funding malaria grant is $165.8 million for ACTs, RDTs, and maintenance of ITN strategy. In Zanzibar, the Global Fund approved budget for malaria was $14.4 million out of which $12 million was disbursed to ZMCP. The future three-year Global Fund Round 8 phase II funding is $5.2 million to cover procurement of ITNs, RDTs, ACTs, and some surveillance and behavior change and communication activities.

PMI, the Global Fund, the British Department for International Development (DFID), the Embassy of the Kingdom of the Netherlands, and the Swiss Agency for Development and Cooperation provide funding for ITN strategy on Mainland and Zanzibar. The Global Fund and PMI co-funded the universal coverage campaign on the Mainland that distributed over 27 million free nets, achieving net coverage of over 91%. In Zanzibar, DFID and the Global Fund procured 727,000 ITNs for the universal coverage campaign and PMI provided funding for the distribution of nets and a net hang-up campaign to improve net use.

The Global Fund, PMI and DFID have shared responsibility in funding the Tanzania National Voucher Scheme that offers ITNs to pregnant women and infants at a highly subsidized fee of

---

[1] Ministry of Health and Social Welfare, United Republic of Tanzania 2011. Tanzania National Health Accounts year 2010 with Sub-Accounts for HIV and AIDS, Malaria, reproductive, and Child Health.
[2] Zanzibar Malaria Strategic Plan 11 (2012-2017)

$0.34. The Global Fund funded the initiative from 2004-2011, PMI funded the initiative from 2006-2013 and in October 2013 DFID will take over the funding of the entire voucher scheme for another two years. The Swiss provide technical assistance to the ITN unit of the NMCP while the Embassy of the Netherlands provides funding to USAID to procure nets, RDTs, and SP.

For case management, PMI and the Global Fund provide all funding for ACTs and RDTs for NMCP and ZMCP. In FY 2014, the Global Fund will provide all funds for procuring ACTs and RDTs however, PMI will provide $2 million for ACTs and $1 million for RDTs to place emergency orders in case of delayed release of funds or late delivery of commodities. PMI will also provide technical assistance for quantification, procurement planning, and monitoring of ACTs and RDTs.

Major non-PMI External Sources of Funding for Malaria Control Mainland, 2008-present			
Source	**Amount (millions)**	**Period Covered**	**What is covered**
Global Fund Single Stream of Funding (R7 and R9 consolidated)	$165	July 2013 – June 2016	Improved malaria case management through the use of RDTs and ACTs in the public and private sectors; Improved quality of care in children with severe malaria; Monitoring and evaluation.
Global Fund	$114	May 2013- April 2016	Sustain universal coverage with ITNs; other interventions (to be decided)
Embassy of the Kingdom of Netherlands	$7.0	Dec 2007– May 2011	Developing capacities of local net manufactures to bundle nets with insecticide treatment kits; Tanzania national voucher scheme (added in 2010), and procurement of RDTs and SP
DFID	$27.0	2013–2018	Funding the Tanzanian National Voucher scheme
Swiss Agency for Development & Cooperation	$6.0	2013 – 2018	ITN Cell within NMCP; school-based ITN distribution pilot in Southern Zone

Private Sector
Through the Global Fund, the Clinton Foundation has provided technical assistance to NMCP and ZMCP to introduce ACT and RDTs, respectively, in the private sector. In FY 2012, PMI partnered with Geita Gold Mine to spray houses in two districts of Geita Region. Geita Gold Mine is providing funds to the local government for operational costs while PMI is providing the insecticide and technical expertise for microplanning, environmental compliance, data management and reporting, and final disposal of chemical waste. In FY 2014, the IRS partnership will expand to cover all the five districts in Geita Region.

Collaboration within the Global Health Initiative and other USG Programs
PMI functions within the GHI strategy and contributes to strengthening health systems for delivery of GHI programs of maternal, neonatal and child health, and reproductive health. At community level, malaria community-based interventions like net distribution, hang-up campaigns, and house spraying use the community change agents and other health workers that deliver a package of other GHI initiatives, such as community based drug distribution for neglected tropical diseases, immunization, and behavior change communication for positive health behaviors.

Collaboration with Other USG Programs
PMI works in collaboration with President's Emergency Plan for AIDS Relief (PEPFAR) on many cross-cutting programmatic issues related to HIV/AIDS and malaria interventions. This has included co-funding two *Tanzania HIV/AIDS and Malaria Indicator Surveys* (THMIS), in 2007 and 2011; co-funding a two-year surveillance officer position in Zanzibar that assisted both

the ZMCP and Zanzibar AIDS Control Program to strengthen surveillance activities and help coordinate disease cluster investigations (FY2011-2012); and co-funding, since 2007, the Tanzania Field Epidemiology & Laboratory Training Program (FELTP). PMI's support for strengthening malaria diagnostics uses the infrastructure and equipment supplied by PEPFAR. The alignment of PEPFAR and malaria diagnostics activities has avoided duplication of efforts and facilitated the mutual interest in developing and implementing appropriate laboratory quality assurance/quality control (QA/QC) programs.

PMI has also partnered with the Department of Defense Walter Reed Army Institute of Research (WRAIR) to strengthen the NMCP and ZMCP malaria diagnostics QA/QC system. PMI also supports Peace Corps Volunteers to develop their capacities for malaria control and promote behavior change communication activities aimed at improving use of ITNs and promotion of early health seeking behavior.

4. PMI GOALS, TARGETS, AND INDICATORS

The goal of PMI is to reduce malaria-associated mortality by 70% in Tanzania compared to pre-Initiative levels. PMI will assist Tanzania to achieve the following targets among persons at risk for malaria:

- More than 90% of households with a pregnant woman and/or children under five will own at least one ITN;
- At least 85% of children under five will have slept under an ITN the previous night;
- At least 85% of pregnant women will have slept under an ITN the previous night;
- At least 85% of houses in geographic areas targeted for IRS will have been sprayed;
- At least 85% of pregnant women and children under five will have slept under an ITN the previous night or in a house that has been sprayed with IRS in the last 12 months.

5. PROGRESS ON COVERAGE AND IMPACT INDICATORS

Four nationally representative population-based household surveys and other data sources provide intervention coverage estimates for key malaria outcome indicators between 2004 and 2012. The table below describes current estimates of intervention coverage and impact indicators, respectively, for the Mainland and Zanzibar. The 2004-05 Tanzania DHS provides baseline estimates for the main PMI indicators of interest.

The 2011-12 THMIS collected data on knowledge and behavior regarding HIV/AIDS and malaria and measured HIV prevalence among adults aged 15-49 and malaria parasitemia among children aged 6-59 months. It also updated estimates of selected demographic and health indicators covered in previous surveys so as to improve calibration of annual sentinel surveillance data and to more accurately measure trends in malaria infection.

Coverage Indicators								
	Mainland				Zanzibar			
Coverage Indicator	2004-05 DHS (%)	2007-08 MIS (%)	2009-10 DHS (%)	2011-12 MIS (%)	2004-05 DHS (%)	2007-08 MIS (%)	2009-10 DHS (%)	2011-12 MIS (%)
Households with at least one ITN	23	38	63	91	28	72	76	74
Children under five who slept under an ITN the previous night	16	25	64	73	22	59	55	51
Pregnant women who slept under an ITN the previous night	15	26	57	76	20	51	50	36
Women who received two or more doses of IPTp at ANC visits during their last pregnancy	22	30	27	33	14	52	47	48
Children under five years old with fever in last two weeks who received any antimalarial treatment.	58	57	60	55	61	66	17	1.7
Children under five years old with fever in the last two weeks who received treatment with ACTs within 24 hours of onset fever.	-	14	27	21	-	9	4	1
Targeted houses adequately sprayed with a residual insecticide in the last 12 months	-	xx[†]	95	-	-	94	96	87

Impact Indicators								

	Mainland				Zanzibar			
Impact Indicator	2004-05 DHS	2007-08 MIS	2000-10 DHS	2011-12 MIS	2004-05 DHS	2007-08 MIS	2009-10 DHS	2011-12 MIS
All-cause under 5 mortality rate	112	92	81	-	101	79	73	-
Parasitemia prevalence (6-59 mo. old)	-	18.1%	-	9%	-	0.8%	-	0.2%
Anemia (Hb<8 g/dL) prevalence (6-59 mo. old)	11.1%	7.8%	5.5%	5.6%	6.4%	4.7%	3.8%	4.1%

In 2012 the Roll Back Malaria Partnership released the results of an Impact Evaluation for Mainland Tanzania that concluded that an estimated 63,000 children under five lives have been saved by malaria control interventions since 1999. Zanzibar has begun the process to conduct an Impact Evaluation in 2013.

6. CHALLENGES, OPPORTUNITIES, THREATS

One of the major programmatic challenges to malaria prevention and control in Mainland Tanzania is related to human resource constraints, including staff shortages, a lack of adequately trained malaria officers at the regional and district levels, and the very high turnover rate of Ministry of Health staff, particularly in more peripheral settings. In addition, the weak supply chain management system further jeopardizes ability of the Ministry of Health and the NMCP to deliver malaria prevention and treatment interventions to all health facilities across the Mainland. Finally, weak information systems hamper the ability of the NMCP to monitor malaria control activities and measure progress. Although PMI, other USAID health programs, and other partners are working to address these problems, it is likely to take several years before progress becomes apparent.

Insecticide-treated nets

Both Mainland and Zanzibar can be justifiably proud of the very high levels of ITN ownership and usage that has been achieved in the past two years. The greatest challenge now for the NMCP and ZMCP will be to sustain those levels of ITN ownership and use following the 2011-12 universal coverage campaign on the Mainland and the 2012 campaign on Zanzibar, as IRS is scaled down. Rallying support and funding around large-scale campaigns seems to be easier than sustaining that support and funding for a continuous ITN distribution system over several years. However, the NMCP has already embarked on a pilot to distribute nets through a school-based system. Furthermore, the Global Fund has agreed to provide an additional $114 million in malaria funding for the Mainland and the Zanzibar malaria grants, so funding gaps for commodities should be minimal for the next two to three years at least.

IRS

IRS continues to benefit from strong political support in both the Mainland and Zanzibar in the face of major reductions in the prevalence of malaria on the Mainland and extremely low levels of transmission on Zanzibar. In fact, both the NMCP and ZMCP have expressed concerns about scaling down IRS coverage, even with very high levels of ITN ownership. Based on currently available evidence, it makes sense to gradually withdraw spraying once transmission levels have been reduced by multiple rounds of IRS and ITN ownership is high. Support for IRS then can be moved to other high prevalence areas. An ongoing PMI-funded study in Lake Zone should help to confirm the validity of this approach. The greatest threat to IRS is the intensification and spread of insecticide resistance, which increases costs of spraying due to more expensive insecticides and necessitates spraying twice a year since most other classes of insecticides have a shorter active duration than the long-acting pyrethroid insecticides.

Diagnosis and Treatment

With the increased Global Fund contributions and continuing PMI support, commodity gaps for RDTs, microscopy supplies, and ACTs are not likely to be a major problem for the next several years. However, continuing to scale up laboratory diagnosis of malaria with microscopy and RDTs will be a major challenge on the Mainland with the continuing problems related to supply chain management, the frequent stockouts of RDTs and ACTs at the health facility level, the large geographic area involved, and the large number of health facilities and health workers who need to be trained, re-trained, or visited for supervision. A training curriculum has been developed as well as a quality control/quality assurance system for RDTs and microscopy, but they now need to be scaled up nationwide.

Malaria in Pregnancy

ANC attendance, which has been high in Tanzania, seems to be falling in recent years. The primary factors contributing to missed opportunities to ensure that all pregnant women receive two doses of sulfadoxine-pyrimethamine (SP) are: a confusing policy related to eligibility for IPTp (by specific weeks); a fifty percent decline in attendance of 4+ ANC visits when the second dose can be administered; a lack of good information in the community regarding efficacy and safety of SP; and repeated stockouts of SP at the ANCs. While health workers' confusion around when to administer SP and pregnant women and their spouses' concerns about the safety of SP during pregnancy cannot be dismissed, shortages of SP are, in fact, a major limiting factor to the scale up of IPTp. A weak supply chain management system, compounded by inadequate communications between programs and Medical Stores Department, has led to stockouts of SP at many health facilities; additionally Reproductive and Child Health supplies and services are generally less financially attractive at the point of service since these services are free and the drugs are to be dispensed without cost recovery. Finally, the misuse of SP for the treatment of suspected malaria during periods of ACT shortage has resulted in the exhaustion of finite SP supplies intended for preventive use in pregnant women. The renewed attention to this problem by the NMCP and partners is encouraging. If Tanzania can promptly adopt the new WHO recommendations related to the timing of IPTp doses, PMI and other partners are ready to support the nationwide rollout of training, follow-up supervision, and community mobilization around malaria in pregnancy. In addition, efforts are already being made with PMI support to improve quantification and distribution of SP to health facilities.

7. PMI SUPPORT STRATEGY

PMI collaborates and coordinates with the NMCP, ZMCP and other partners based upon the NMCP's and ZMCP's strategic goals and priorities. The level of support for each of the interventions takes into consideration the contributions from other donors such as the Government of Tanzania, the Global Fund, DFID, and other stakeholders to ensure priority interventions are scaled up to fill gaps, avoid duplication, and target interventions to address regional variations in malaria epidemiology and progress to date.

Mainland Tanzania's goal is malaria control and prevention, focusing certain interventions on areas with the highest transmission and others on routine malaria prevention. For instance, IRS is supported in the Lake Zone, the area with the highest transmission, while ITNs are universally distributed throughout the Mainland.

In Zanzibar, decreasing malaria prevalence has prompted the ZMCP to adopt a new malaria 2014-2020 strategy, which focuses on achieving pre-elimination by 2018. They are reevaluating their interventions to match the current epidemiology and PMI is supporting these changes. For instance, they are scaling down IRS from blanket spraying to focusing on hot spots and they are changing their Malaria in Pregnancy strategy to match the lowered prevalence (see MIP sections for details). PMI is supporting the ZMCP to realign their interventions and is working with the ZMCP to ensure rationale strategies are adopted relating to the changing epidemiology.

OPERATIONAL PLAN

1. INSECTICIDE-TREATED NETS

NMCP/ZMCP/PMI Objectives
Mainland
The NMCP objective is to achieve and maintain universal access of long lasting insecticide-treated nets (ITNs) in order to have at least 80% appropriate use by 2020. NMCP's ITN strategy is to: 1) implement a mass ITN distribution campaign if access drops below a threshold of 60%; 2) use a "keep-up strategy" to maintain high access to ITNs; 3) re-establish a viable commercial market for ITNs in Tanzania; and, 4) promote appropriate use of ITNs. NMCP defines universal coverage as one net per sleeping space. The ITN strategy addresses gender and equity disparities through the voucher ITN scheme that targets pregnant women and infants, and a free mass net distribution campaigns that provides nets to the general population at no cost to the beneficiaries.

In order to achieve high ITN coverage, the NMCP has supported several different programs:
- A national voucher scheme-aimed at providing nets to pregnant women and infants at ANC clinic.
- An "Under-Five Catch-up Campaign" (U5CC) to distribute free ITNs to all children under five.
- A "Universal Coverage Campaign" (UCC) to distribute free ITNs for all remaining household sleeping spaces to cover the entire population.

In 2011, the Mainland achieved universal coverage of nets. A keep-up net strategy assessment took place shortly afterwards to look at how Tanzania could maintain universal coverage. Several distribution channels were recommended. Based on those recommendations, the NCMP has been revising its ITN keep-up/replacement strategy. While the goal of 80% coverage remains the same, the distribution channels being considered are a combination of: 1) an expansion of school-based net distribution to 10 regions, covering 30% of the population; 2) a mass replacement campaign in the remaining 15 regions, and 3) maintaining the Tanzania National Voucher Scheme (TNVS) to provide nets to the pregnant women and newborn infants. The MOP will be revised to reflect this change. Each of these interventions is described below.

School-based net distribution (SN).: The school-based net project distributes free nets to school children in first, third, fifth, seventh, ninth, and eleventh grades. Ten districts will be chosen, covering 30% of the population, Districts chosen will be those that are not included in the mass replacement campaign. The school-based net (SN) distribution is a new channel for net distribution, but not the only channel planned in Tanzania. A pilot SN distribution is currently ongoing and preliminary results of the final evaluation will be available in September 2013. These results will guide the final strategy.

Mass replacement campaign: The mass replacement campaign will take place in the 15 regions with the oldest nets and with suboptimal net access (percentage of population with less than a net per two people). The selection of regions for this campaign will be based on age of the net, access to ITNs, and malaria prevalence.

Tanzania National Voucher Scheme (TNVS):. The TNVS began in November 2004 with support from the Global Fund to improve the availability of ITNs to pregnant women through a subsidized voucher scheme. In 2006, PMI supported the expansion of the TNVS to infants. Under the TNVS, vouchers are issued at health facilities offering antenatal and child health services and redeemed at a retail shop where the pregnant woman or infant caretaker exchanges the voucher, along with a top-up fee (which the retailer keeps), for a net. Net manufacture and distribution are fully-funded by donors and the private sector, so there is no cost to the retailer. The top-up fee provides an incentive for the retailer to participate in the program. The voucher scheme operates through a network of more than 6,000 retailers. To improve net retailer participation, PMI and the local net manufacturer provided a net subsidy whereby PMI and the local net manufacturer provided five LLINs each to the participating net retailer, on condition that the net retailer purchases five LLINs out of pocket. Together, these 15 LLINs capitalize the private sector market and maintain a strong and sustainable retail network. In essence, this allows the retailer to earn $0.30 for every net redeemed. To date, over 9 million nets have been distributed through the TNVS since 2004, out of which 4.6 million are LLINs.

Tanzania mainland has distributed 31.5 million LLINs— 4.6 million through the TNVS, 8.7 million through the U5CC, and 18.2 million through the UCC. The 2011/12 THMIS shows high ITN ownership of 91%, ranging from 85-96%.

Zanzibar

ZMCP objective is to maintain over 80% ITN coverage. The ITN strategy is a combination of: 1) free net distribution to pregnant women during ANC visits and to children under the age of five during vaccinations at child health clinics; 2) distribution of ITNs at village level (_shehias_) on demand to replace the unusable nets; and 3) social marketing of ITNs at the open market price. ZMCP has been distributing free ITNs to pregnant women and infants since 2006 via ANC clinics and child vaccination clinics. In 2008, ZMCP altered its net distribution strategy to provide two free ITNs per household, but the ZMCP now defines universal coverage as up to three nets per household. The 2011/12 THMIS showed a declining household ITN ownership to 74% in 2011 from 76% in 2010, and in usage to 51% from 55% for children under five and to 36% from 50% for pregnant women sleeping under an ITN. The results motivated ZMCP to implement a universal coverage campaign in 2012.

To improve net use, PMI, in partnership with DFID, supported NMCP to conduct a hang-up campaign after the Mainland U5CC and UCC. PMI supported another net hang-up campaign in Zanzibar after their UCC. The timing of the campaigns was one month after ITN distribution. Trained volunteers visited every household to ensure that nets were properly hung, and educated communities to sleep under a net every night.

Net use for Zanzibar is low at 44% for households, 51% for under-five children, and 36% for pregnant women (2011/12 THMIS), but these results preceded the March 2012 Zanzibar universal coverage and hang up campaigns. Although Zanzibar net coverage and use was low in 2011 when the survey took place, 95% of household members slept under an ITN the night before the survey or in a house sprayed with IRS in the last 12 months (2011/12 THMIS).

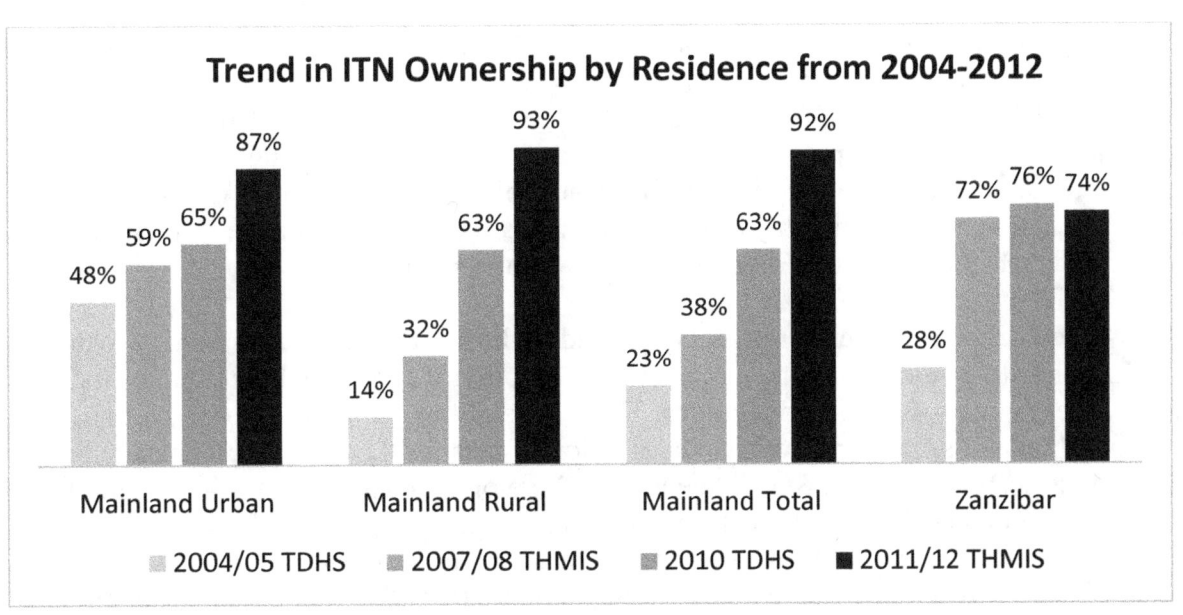

Trend in ITN Ownership by Residence from 2004-2012

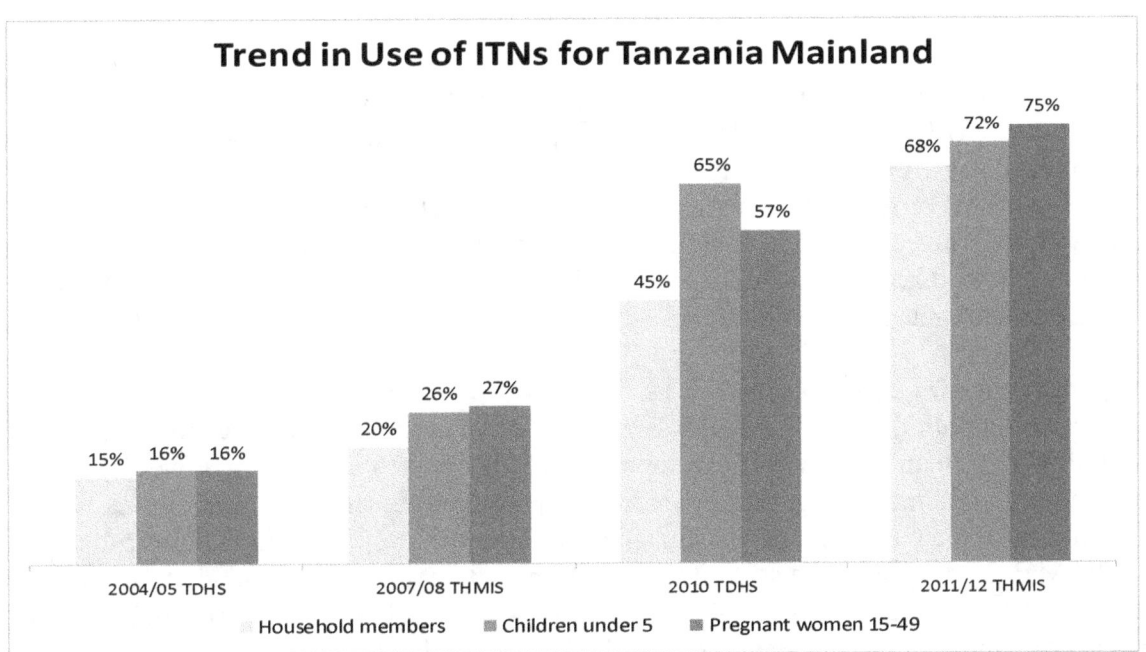

Trend in Use of ITNs for Tanzania Mainland

Progress in the Past 12 Months
Mainland

The Mainland is piloting an ITN keep-up strategy that will sustain the availability and use of nets at an affordable cost. The keep-up strategy is a combination of: 1) the school-based net distribution; and 2) the voucher scheme for the pregnant women and infants. It is expected that this combined keep-up net program could distribute approximately 8 million nets per year, allowing for the Mainland to maintain 90% net coverage in the wake of the U5CC and UCC.

The paper-based voucher system was switched to an electronic voucher (eVoucher) in most regions, which helped to improve the efficiency, choice, and competition for the vouchers. The eVoucher shortens the time for redemption and reduce costs associated with a paper voucher such as printing costs. The eVoucher is "issued" via cell-phone-based SMS technology and is automatically voided after 60 days if the voucher is not redeemed at a participating retailer, enabling the implementer to issue more vouchers. Besides cutting operational costs, it is expected that the eVoucher will provide geospatial data on voucher use throughout the Mainland, helping to better target BCC efforts. It is expected that choice and competition will stimulate the private market, and foster sustainability as those who can afford it will buy a net of their own choice (size and color) at full price. However, this is yet to be evaluated.

The school-based net project is currently being piloted in the Southern Zone, covering the three regions of Lindi, Mtwara, and Ruvuma. Free nets will be provided to school children in first, third, fifth, seventh, ninth, and eleventh grades. The results of this pilot will inform the final design of the Mainland's keep-up strategy. Distribution of nets for the SN will commence in May 2013 and is co-funded by the Swiss Agency for Development and Cooperation. Using FY 2012 funds, PMI procured 510,000 ITNs for the pilot and supported the local Tanzanian Red Cross Society to transport and distribute nets to schools. The strategy will be evaluated in July 2013 and preliminary results will be available in September 2013. The results will shape the future planning for this activity.

Zanzibar
The ZMCP implemented their first universal coverage campaign between January and March 2012 and distributed 727,000 ITNs (one to three ITNs per household). This was direct result of the low net coverage shown in 2011/12 THMIS. The Global Fund procured 220,000 nets and DFID 507,000 nets. PMI provided funding for registration, distribution to the issuing sites, and actual issuing of nets. The campaign used more than 2,000 Tanzania Red Cross Society-trained volunteers who registered households, issued nets to households, and made follow-up visits to homes to ensure that all nets had been hung.

Challenges, opportunities, and threats
The ITN programs on both the Mainland and Zanzibar receive combined funding from the Global Fund, PMI, DfID, and the Swiss Development Agency and Corporation. However, these programs are highly vulnerable because they mainly rely on funding from external donors with minimal funding from the Government of Tanzania. The delay in designing an ITN keep-up strategy on the Mainland delayed the start of the school based net pilot, and is likely to affect the implementation of the planned ITN strategy for FY 2013 and FY 2014FY 2014. Disposal of old and unusable nets remains an unresolved issue for both Mainland and Zanzibar.

The short longevity of ITNs (less than three years) is a challenge for NMCP and ZMCP. When PMI support started, net life was expected to be four to five years and initial budget plans were based on these numbers. Now that net life is shorter, increased funding is needed to cover the gap. The unpredictable release of Global Fund money and condition precedents are some of the challenges NMCP and ZMCP face in accessing funding for the ITN strategy on time.

The biggest threat to the ITN strategy is insecticide resistance. Most recent 2012 data shows that insecticide resistance to pyrethroids used on ITNs is spreading very fast, threatening the ITN strategy. Longitudinal entomological monitoring has shown that *An. gambiae ss* is predominantly endophilic and has decreased in Zanzibar, having been replaced by the exophilic and exophagic *An. arabiensis.* The same vector bionomics is being observed on Mainland where *An. arabiensis* is becoming more dominant, threatening both ITNs and IRS.

ITN Gap analysis

NETCALC modeling shows that the Mainland will need 26.6 million ITNs for three years (2014-2016) to bring household ownership and access to 2011 levels out of which 1.3 million are expected to be distributed through the TNVS annually, 510,400 nets through school-based net distribution annually, and the remaining 20.9 million will be distributed through a targeted mass replacement campaign.

ITN Gap Analysis-Mainland

	Total	2013	2014	2015
Projected Target Populations				
Annual Projected population		44,803,239	46,012,926	47,255,275
Population targeted for school-based distribution for 3 regions	2,756,160	918,720	918,720	918,720
Population targeted for mass replacement campaign in remaining 22 regions, assuming 90% coverage, based on 2013 population projections	40,112,957	7,870,244	18,067,500	14,175,213
Pregnant women (4.9%)		2,195,359	2,254,633	2,315,508
Number of surviving infants (4.7%)		2,105,752	2,162,608	2,220,998
ITN needs by Distribution Channel				
ITNs through SN distribution channel assuming	1,531,200	510,400	510,400	510,400
ITNs for Mass replacement campaign	20,906,120	4,372,358	14,973,184	1,560,578
ITNs for pregnant women assuming 50% coverage & 70% redemption rate	2,131,133	691,538	710,210	729,385
ITNs for infants, assuming 50% coverage and 70% redemption rate	2,044,148	663,312	681,221	699,614
Total ITNs needed from July 2013 -June 2016	26,612,600	6,237,608	16,875,015	3,499,978
Available funds and ITN gap				
ITNs with available funding	DfID up to April 2014 - (2,354,850)	1,354,850	1,000,000	0
	Global Fund - (18,800,000)	4,372,358	12,167,450	2,260,192
	PMI FY 2012 & FY 2013 funds (4,217,965)	510,400	3,707,565	0
ITN Gap		0	0	1,239,785

ITN Gap Analysis: Zanzibar

	Year	
	2014	**2015**
Population Estimates		
Population in Zanzibar	1,377,591	1,416,164
Number of pregnant women (4.5%)	67,502	69,392
Number of surviving infants (4.3%)	64,747	66,560
ITN Needs		
Annual net replacement need (at target of 100%)	243,586	250,406
ANC+EPI+Community(equivalent to >90% annual ITN requirement)	**221,859**	**228,159**
Distribution Channels		
ANC (assuming 80% ANC attendance and >80% ITN coverage)	49,384	50,915
EPI (assuming 80% EPI attendance and >80% ITN coverage)	41,334	42,038
Community (53% of households/year)	131,141	135,206
Available Funding and ITN Gap		
ITNs covered from available funding (Global Fund)	221,859	228,159
ITN gap	0	0

- *Source: Gap analysis based on Zanzibar ITN Continuous Distribution Strategy*
- **Projections based on 2012 population census with GR of 2.8%*

Plans and Justification
Mainland
PMI will contribute to the NCMP ITN keep-up strategy by providing over $8 million for the purchase of nets for the SN program and procurement and distribution of 2.1 million nets for the replacement strategy in two regions—Kagera and Kigoma. PMI funds will also be used to procure approximately 290,000 nets for pregnant women and infants in the SN program regions in calendar year 2015 when DfID funding for the voucher scheme ends in April 2015. The Global Fund is providing $114 million for the procurement of 18.8 million ITNs over a period of three years—July 2013 to June 2016, and is targeting a mass replacement campaign in the non-PMI 21 regions. Global Fund and PMI money will cover the total costs for these two channels of distribution while DFID will fund the voucher scheme starting in October 2013 through April 2015.

Zanzibar
Zanzibar achieved universal ITN coverage in March 2012. In FY 2014, the Global Fund will procure all the 233,400 nets required for the continuous net distribution. PMI will use some FY 2013 funds to support the distribution of the nets and improve net use through the net hang-up campaign.

Budget and Proposed Activities with FY 2014 Funding
Mainland
With FY 2014 funding, PMI plans to procure up to 1.4 million ITNs as contribution towards the ITN keep-up strategy for Tanzania Mainland. In the event that Global Fund money can be used for distribution costs, PMI will reprogram this money towards other NMCP activities. *($8,243,500)*

Zanzibar
PMI will use some of its FY 2013 funds to support the distribution of the nets and improve net use through the net hang-up campaign. *($0)*

2. INDOOR RESIDUAL SPRAYING

NMCP/ZMCP/PMI Objectives
Mainland
The NMCP's 2008-2013 Medium-Term Strategic Plan targets IRS in areas of high malaria prevalence and unstable transmission. When IRS started on the Mainland in 2007, the Lake Zone regions had the highest burden of malaria among all 21 regions of the Mainland. Malaria prevalence among children 6-59 months of age was 41% in Kagera, 31% in Mwanza, and 30% in Mara (2007-08 THMIS). The 2014-2020 Strategic Plan has not yet been finalized, but the NCMP goal is to scale-down IRS in areas with low malaria prevalence and high ITN coverage and to assure continued high coverage of ITNs.

Using 2007/08 THMIS data, IRS was targeted in the Lake Zone, starting with the Kagera region which had the highest malaria prevalence (41%) in 2007. After five to six rounds of IRS, there was a dramatic drop in malaria prevalence to 9% (2011/12 THMIS). PMI and NMCP are using the recent 2011/12 THMIS data to scale down and deploy IRS in areas with high malaria prevalence. IRS has been scaled down in Kagera region and will end with FY 2012 funds. Kagera region will be replaced with Geita Region, which currently has the highest malaria prevalence of 32% (2011/12 THMIS). If funds allow, IRS will be scaled up to Kigoma Region which has a malaria prevalence of 26%. With this change, IRS will be implemented only in regions with the highest malaria prevalence, except for the Lindi Region because it is benefiting from the school-based ITN pilot.

Since 2007, the NCMP has sprayed 18 districts in Lake Zone. Data from 2010 THMIS shows that the Lake Zone had the highest under-five mortality rate of 109/1,000 live births, above the national average of 81/1,000 live births. In late 2011 and early 2012, based on evidence of increasing insecticide resistance, the PMI-supported IRS strategy in the Lake Zone was changed. A carbamate insecticide (bendiocarb) was used for Kagera and certain areas in Mwanza and Mara regions, while the remaining areas were sprayed with a pyrethroid. In addition, targeted spraying was initiated in the Muleba district.

IRS Coverage and Number of People Protected on Mainland							
Region	Number of Districts	Round	Year	Structures sprayed	Coverage	People protected	Insecticide used
Kagera	1 (Muleba)	1	2006/07	34,745	94.9%	167,871	Pyrethroid
Kagera	2 (Muleba & Karagwe)	2	2007/08	95,548	98.6%	448,690	Pyrethroid
Kagera	2 (Muleba & Karagwe)	3	2008/09	185,217	96.3%	872,378	Pyrethroid
Kagera	All 7 districts	4	2009/10	425,118	96.2%	2,138,299	Pyrethroid
Kagera, Mwanza, Mara	All 18 districts	5	2010/11	1,144,621	94.5%	6,343,091	Pyrethroid
Kagera, Mwanza, Mara	All 18 districts	6	2011/12	1,224,095	93.2%	6,518,120	Carbamate in Muleba & Karagwe; Pyrethroid in rest of 16 districts
Kagera, Mwanza, Mara	*Targeted spraying in 18 districts	7	2012/13	655,024	95.8%	3,65546	• Carbamate in Kagera region and 3 districts of Mwanza and 2 districts in Mara regions • Pyrethroid in rest of districts of Mwanza & Mara regions

*Data for the second round of targeted spraying with carbamates in 2012/13 is expected end June 2013

Zanzibar

The Zanzibar malaria elimination goal is to achieve 100% coverage with IRS or ITNs by 2015 by achieving 95% coverage of IRS in the target areas, and 90% ITN use in non-IRS areas. The ZMCP strategy has been to scale-down IRS over recent years in line with reduced malaria prevalence. The strategy was to conduct blanket (all sprayable structures in the island) spraying in all ten districts in Zanzibar, then move to target spraying in only the districts showing high malaria transmission, then scale IRS down further to focal spraying of hot spots (catchment areas with 2 cases/1,000 population) once malaria transmission became localized. Zanzibar moved from blanket to targeted spraying in 2011, and then to focal spraying early 2013.

The original plan was to move from blanket to focal spraying over a period of nine to ten years (see figure below). However, with the achievement of universal coverage with ITNs and dramatic reduction in malaria prevalence to 0.2%, the scale-down of IRS in Zanzibar through the three phases was accelerated.

IRS Scale-down plan

Spray phase	2006 - 2007	2007- 2008	2008- 2009	2009- 2010	2010- 2011	2011- 2012	2012- 2013	2013- 2014	2014- 2015
Blanket (Knock-down)									
Targeted (Keep-down)									
Focal (Keep-low)									

— **Blanket** *to knock-down transmission (or knock-down further) in entire regions*
— **Targeted** *to maintain low transmission in particular districts with high/increasing transmission*
— **Focal** *to address specific "hot spots" where higher transmission persists*

From 2006 to early 2013, Zanzibar has benefited from six rounds of blanket IRS, two rounds of targeted IRS, and three focal spraying of hot spots and malaria outbreak areas. At each round, household coverage of over 90% has been achieved. Because of the changing malaria epidemiology in Zanzibar, coupled with a robust and reliable surveillance and entomological monitoring system, Zanzibar moved from blanket to targeted spraying in 2011 when the seventh round of spraying covered eight of the ten districts. Focal IRS was conducted between June 26 and July 4 2008 in Bumbwini (North B district), Zanzibar targeted five villages in response to an abnormal increase in malaria cases identified through the newly introduced MEEDS. In 2011, focal spraying was also used in the malaria hot spots in Uzi and Jadele districts. Focal spraying as an IRS scale-down strategy for Zanzibar started in 2011. In 2012, Zanzibar further reduced the areas for IRS, targeting areas showing increased malaria transmission. A mapping exercise using epidemiological data from 142 health facilities was used to map villages (*shehias*) showing increased malaria transmission. The *shehias* showing malaria incidence of more than 2 cases/1,000 population were eligible for IRS. In early 2013, Zanzibar moved to focal spraying of only hot spots.

Round		Year	Structures sprayed	Coverage	No. of people protected	Insecticide used
Round 1		2006	203,754	96%	1,059,521	Pyrethroid
Round 2		2007	196,827	90%	1,023,500	Pyrethroid
Round 3		2007	212,021	97%	1,102,609	Pyrethroid
Focal spraying		2008	3,588	100%	18,658	Pyrethroid
Round 4		2008	200,731	94%	1,067,254	Pyrethroid
Round 5		2010	183,620	89%	1,019,921	Pyrethroid
Round 6		2011	194,808	95%	1,033,742	Pyrethroid
Round 7	Targeted 8/10 districts	2012	114,858	95%	689,148	Carbamate
	Focal		26,270	95%	126,552	
Round 8	Targeted	2013	49,640	96%	240,853	Carbamate
	*Focal					

*Focal spraying data is expected end June 2013

Progress in the Past 12 Months
Mainland
The Mainland reduced the targeted area for IRS from 1.32 million to 838,000 structures, targeting areas that had received fewer than four rounds of IRS. A total of 655,024 structures were sprayed with over 90% coverage, protecting over 3.4 million people. Based on WHO guidance, the NMCP has adopted a strategy of insecticide rotation prior to development of resistance. The spraying in the last 12 months used both carbamates in Kagera region and three districts of Mwanza where insecticide resistance to pyrethroids had been detected. The rest of Mwanza Region and Mara Region that had only two rounds of IRS were sprayed with pyrethroids as sensitivity was greater than 90%. The areas sprayed with carbamates received two rounds of spraying at the time of the two transmission seasons.

Over the last year, PMI, NMCP, and ZMCP have actively engaged with key partners and stakeholders towards development of a long-term insecticide resistance mitigation plan for Tanzania that will guide the rational choice and use of insecticides for IRS. Stakeholders deliberated using alternate classes of insecticide, including Actellic CS, and included these in the interim insecticide resistance mitigation plan. Initial challenges were registration of such products in Mainland Tanzania, where regulations differ from Zanzibar, and the high cost. However, with the scale-down of IRS in the Lake Zone and Zanzibar, and with the rotation of insecticide from pyrethroids to carbamates, plans are underway to move to other formulations, like Actellic CS. In Zanzibar, the testing of Actellic CS has begun.

Zanzibar
Zanzibar implemented a combination of targeted and focal spraying. Targeted spraying took place in 2012 in the districts that showed increased malaria transmission. The targeted spraying covered 114,858 structures (95% coverage) and protected 689,148 people. The focal spraying in

the hot spots started at the end of 2012 and 26,270 structures were sprayed, protecting126,552 people. In February 2013, another round of targeted spraying took place in the villages (*shehias*) that showed malaria incidence of more than 2 cases/1,000 population. Targeted spraying took place in 49,640 structures, protecting 240,853 people. In the last 12 months, carbamate was used for IRS.

IRS activities in the Mainland and Zanzibar ensure protection of the environment and safe disposal of waste in accordance with the approved Pesticide Evaluation Report and Safe Use Action Plans. Environmental inspection visits are conducted regularly to assess compliance with US Government and Tanzanian national environmental standards.

IRS Gap Analysis
The IRS gap analysis below is for targeted spraying on Mainland based on two to three rounds of spraying using bendiocarb, which is three times more expensive than lambda-cyhalothrin CS 10% and has a shorter residual effect. Zanzibar will have only focal spraying in FY 2014 and will be changing to the long-lasting Actellic insecticide in 2013.

IRS target areas	IRS strategy (blanket, targeted, focal)		Number of targeted structures		Population to be protected		Type of insecticide		Total Budget	
	FY 2013	FY 2014	FY 2013	FY 2014	FY 2013	FY 2014	FY 2013	FY 2014	FY 2013	FY 2014
Kagera	Focal	None	70,667	-	393,284	-	Actellic	None	1,766,675	0
Mara	Targeted	Focal	190,181	69,618	1,098,613	277,862	Vectron	Actellic	3,042,896	1,740,450
Mwanza	Targeted	Focal	206,435	89,504	1,746,681	441,772	Vectron	Actellic	3,302,960	2,237,600
Geita	Blanket	Blanket	293,154	296,554	1,788,237	1,836,519	Vectron	Vectron	4,690,464	4,744,864
Kigoma	None	Blanket	-	393,774	-	2,187,512	None	Vectron	-	6,300,384
Mainland			760,437	849,450	5,026,815	4,743,665			12,802,995	15,023,298
Zanzibar	Focal	Focal	21,985	20,207	110,803	101,845	Actellic	Actellic	549,625	505,175

- *Frequency of spray using Actellic CS and Vectron will be one round, covering both malaria transmission periods*
- *Unit costs per structure sprayed, including operational costs: $25 for Actellic CS and $16 for Vectron*
- *Geita Gold mine will contribute $200,000 towards operational costs of spraying in Geita Region leaving a funding gap of $14,823,298*

Challenges, opportunities, and threats
Achieving universal coverage with ITNs on Mainland and Zanzibar provided an opportunity and justification to scale down IRS and instead, strengthen ITN strategy availability and use to sustain the gains made in vector control. Public-private partnerships, such as partnering with Geita Gold Mine, provides an opportunity to expand IRS to target the Geita Region.

Data from 2012 show that insecticide resistance to pyrethroids is spreading very rapidly, threatening the effectiveness of both ITNs and IRS. This is compounded by the limited choice of insecticides for IRS that are WHOPES approved and registered locally by the Tanzania insecticide regulatory authority. The alternatives to the currently used pyrethroids for IRS are expensive and have a shorter residual action. In addition, carbamates, which are being used in some Mainland districts and all of Zanzibar, are about three times as expensive as pyrethroids, with higher associated operational costs.

Longitudinal entomological monitoring has shown that the population of endophilic *An. gambiae ss* has declined in Zanzibar and been replaced by the exophilic and exophagic *An. arabiensis*. The same change is being observed on Mainland where *An. arabiensis* is becoming more dominant in IRS target area, threatening both ITNs and IRS.

Plans and Justification for FY 2014
Mainland
PMI is the only donor funding IRS in Tanzania. With the achievement of universal coverage with ITNs, the marked reduction of malaria prevalence from 41% in 2007 (2007/08 THMIS) to 9% in 2012 (2011/12 THMIS), and the reduction in the number of reported malaria cases over the past four years, PMI and NMCP decided to scale-down IRS in the Kagera Region and focus on continued ITN availability and use. The team will closely monitor the region via entomologic and epidemiologic surveillance to assess if there is a change in malaria transmission after withdrawal of IRS. In addition, the NMCP will stock additional ACT medicines and RDTs in the region in the event of an increase of malaria cases. At the same time, the NMCP is scaling up IRS in the Geita Region.

The IRS budget also includes conducting environmental supplemental assessments and development of pesticide evaluation report and safe use action plans (PERSUAP) in new areas of IRS expansion; conducting environmental monitoring before, during, and after the spray season; cross border collaboration; final disposal of medical waste; and capacity building for IRS operations.

Cross border collaboration with Uganda, Kenya, Rwanda, and Burundi will involve networking, exchange visits, and regional meetings to share information and best practices for malaria control. Areas of collaboration will start around IRS, entomological monitoring, insecticide resistance monitoring and mitigation plans, selection of insecticides, disease surveillance, and exit plans for IRS.

Zanzibar
In 2012, Zanzibar achieved universal coverage with ITNs and thus began to scale-down IRS. Zanzibar also has a strong entomological and epidemiologic surveillance system that provides real time data for epidemic detection and response. With FY 2014 funding, PMI will support focal spraying in the villages (*shehias*) that will show malaria incidence of more than 2 cases/1,000 population.

Budget and Proposed Activities with FY 2014 Funding

Mainland
PMI will support two rounds of IRS in the 16 districts of Mwanza, Mara and Ngeita Regions, covering 418,900 structures and protecting approximately 2.5 million people. The spraying in Ngeita will be under a public-private partnership with Geita Gold Mine that will contribute approximately $200,000 towards the operational costs of the spraying. PMI will also support activities for cross border collaboration with Uganda, Kenya, Rwanda, and Burundi. (*$14,823,000*)

Zanzibar
PMI will support focal spraying in hot spots, covering 20,207 structures and protecting 101,845 people. ($500,000)

Mainland and Zanzibar
PMI supports activities for environmental compliance and final disposal of empty insecticide sachets, in accordance with US Government and Zanzibar environmental laws (22 CFR 216). There is a pipeline of $70,000 to conduct an independent environmental assessment on Mainland and Zanzibar. (*$0*)

3. MALARIA IN PREGNANCY

NMCP/ZMCP/PMI Objectives
Tanzania utilizes the three-pronged approach to prevent the adverse effects associated with malaria in pregnancy recommended by the WHO: 1) ITNs through antenatal care clinics, 2) provision of intermittent preventative treatment (IPTp) with sulfadoxine-pyrimethamine (SP), and 3) prompt case management of pregnant women with malaria. The objectives for these goals are to achieve 80% coverage of two doses of IPTp, 80% use of ITNs by pregnant women, and 100% prompt case management of malaria infections in pregnancy.

IPTp
Currently, the NMCP and ZMCP are both implementing the three interventions however significant changes are being made to both IPTp policies.

Mainland
The MOHSW is in the process of changing their IPTp policy to reflect updated WHO guidance. The new policy is to give three or more doses of SP as directly observed therapy during ANC visits.

Zanzibar
Currently, the policy for IPTp in Zanzibar is to give two doses of SP during pregnancy and the coverage rate is 48%. However, given the low prevalence of malaria in women at time of delivery (0.8%), and a focus on elimination of malaria, Zanzibar is considering a move away from IPTp and toward intermittent screening and treatment in pregnancy, with screening by RDT at each ANC visit and treatment only if the test is positive. A consultative meeting will convene all relevant stakeholders to make a final determination. The decision will take into account not

only efficacy but also the cost of the various strategies. Regardless of the approach to screening asymptomatic women, all symptomatic women will be screened.

Iron/folate

Tanzanian policy is to give a combination pill containing ferrous sulfate 200mg plus folic acid 0.25 mg once daily throughout pregnancy or, if uncombined, give ferrous sulfate 200mg plus folic acid 1mg once daily throughout pregnancy. However, in practice this is not always available, and in those cases, 5 mg is given instead.

Case management of acute malaria

Case management of malaria in pregnancy follows WHO recommendations. The policy for treatment of severe malaria has been updated, with a switch to use of parenteral artesunate in all cases of severe malaria, including those occurring in pregnant women, regardless of trimester of pregnancy. Health workers are being trained and the new policy is in the process of being implemented.

Progress since PMI started in 2006

Mainland

Until 2012, PMI and maternal health funding focused on rolling out the national training on Focused Antenatal Care (FANC), a package of antenatal services which includes IPTp. Cumulatively, 7,181 providers from 3,540 Mainland facilities have been trained. PMI has also supported development of a pre-service malaria in pregnancy training curriculum, which has contributed to approximately 1,600 new graduates with FANC skills each year since 2006. Training in antenatal care continues when District Health Management Teams invest their own budgets and use PMI-trained trainers to conduct further training within their district.

Although ANC attendance is almost universal (96% of pregnant women make at least one visit; 2010 TDHS), IPTp uptake rates have not markedly improved over time (see table below). Alarmingly, although attendance at the first visit has remained stable, attendance at four visits has fallen from 65% (1999) to 38% (2010). Other factors contributing to poor uptake are: 1) challenging commodity logistics and misuse, 2) poor provider attitude and confusion over timing of administration, 3) insufficient supervision at facility level, and 4) inadequate community awareness of efficacy and safety of SP during pregnancy.

IPTp uptake in Tanzania

Intervention	2004/05 DHS	2007 THMIS	2009/10 DHS	2012 THMIS
Percentage of women who took at least 1 dose of SP at ANC during their last pregnancy (IPTp 1)	53%	57%	60%	60%
Percentage of women who took at least 2 doses of SP at ANC during their last pregnancy (IPTp 2)	21.9%	29.6%	25.7%	33%

Progress during last 12 months

In order to promote the uptake of interventions delivered through ANCs, Tanzania has in the past year revived its Malaria in Pregnancy Task force, a group composed of members from both the NMCP and the Reproductive and Child Health group as well as other relevant stakeholders.

Since November 2012, there has been an integrated campaign aimed at improving uptake of all ANC services, including two doses of SP. This Ministry-led Safe Motherhood Campaign (*Wazazi Nipendeni*) has provided printed materials to over 3,000 clinics across the country including posters as well as SP reminder cards to assist women in remembering when to return for their second dose. Through this multimedia campaign, general health promotion messages are broadcast via TV and radio including information regarding malaria in pregnancy; additionally a pregnant woman can register to receive phone-messages providing her and her partner with useful information related to her trimester of pregnancy, as well as reminders of when her next visit should be. An evaluation of this campaign is planned in November 2013 to serve as a basis of determining the efficacy of this approach and opportunities to expand on the text messaging platform (e.g. sending reminders to providers to reinforce the need for provision of quality care).

The safe motherhood campaign was developed as an integrated umbrella platform that could include a number of health themes for pregnant women and children. This has led to growing interest among health partners to support the platform with a number of messages and activities.

With FY 2012-2013 funds, PMI leveraged other USG funds to develop an integrated supervision system to improve FANC service provision and institutionalize a facility-based quality improvement approach. To date, this has been rolled out in 250 facilities in 115 districts in more than 16 regions across the country, while at the same time empowering district and regional Reproductive and Child Health Coordinators to undertake supervision using the standardized approach.

Following the release of updated WHO guidance in October 2012, the MOHSW convened a MIP Task Force, under the Safe Motherhood Working Group, to conduct a more thorough investigation into the issues related to IPTp uptake and to make recommendations for policy/service delivery changes in order to more effectively bring the intervention to scale. This group has proposed changes to the Tanzanian policy on IPTp to align Tanzania's policy with the revised WHO recommendation and promote three or more doses of IPTp (IPTp3+). Once the recommendations are approved, there is a plan to roll-out this new guidance along with updates on case management. Additional opportunities for dissemination of the new guidelines are also being discussed such as appending a half-day training to the scheduled national rollout of PMTCT trainings. Training materials have been updated to indicate the new guidance and will be rolled out once the new policy is officially approved. In addition, as part of the training on new SP guidelines, a memo will be issued from MOHSW reiterating that SP is provided free to the facility from the medical stores department (MSD), which should increase the demand.

Commodity gap analysis

SP has historically been procured by the Tanzanian government, although a large order was recently procured through funding from the Dutch government by a local partner. Currently it is estimated that there are approximately 23 months stock of SP at the Central Medical Stores warehouse. The Tanzanian government will continue to procure SP when this supply is exhausted; thus PMI has no plans to procure SP. However, there have been persistent challenges in getting this stock to the peripheral facilities. PMI is working to address this problem to ensure availability at facilities with ANC clinics.

NATIONAL STOCK STATUS OF SULPHADOXINE PYRIMENTHAMINE (SP)
Based on quantification exercises conducted in February 2013, the annual requirements for SP assuming coverage of 80% IPTp2 in the next 2 years are provided in the table below:

Commodity	UOM	2013 QTY	2014 QTY	2015 QTY
SP	TAB	9,719,999	9,982,443	10,251,967

The table below provides the stock on hand report for SP at MSD central and zones by the end of May 2013:

Quantity	QUANTITIES (TABS)	Months of Stocks
SP	8,296,810	10

The average monthly consumption (AMC) is 810,000 tabs and therefore the months of stock as end of May, 2013 were 10.2. It is recommended that an additional 3,310,300 tablets will be needed at the end of September, and an additional 5,128,000 tablets will be needed by the end of April 2014. The Government of Tanzania has not placed any orders, although they have committed to ensuring sufficient quantities of SP are available. PMI will continue to monitor the situation, and if needed will reprogram funds to procure SP in order to prevent serious stockouts.

Desired Receive Date	Quantity(tins of 100)	Product Costs	Freight Cost	Total cost
09/28/2013	33,103	$3,972.36	$715.02	$4,687.38
04/31/2014	51,280	$6,153.60	$1,107.65	$7,261.25
TOTAL				$11,948.63

Plans and Justification
Mainland
PMI will support the roll-out of the updated MIP guidance, including supporting training of ANC providers and printing of updated guidelines in the next 18 months. PMI will continue to support the District and Regional Reproductive and Child Health Coordinators to roll out the integrated supervision system to non-supported facilities, focusing on Lindi and Mtwara Regions in 2013, and then expanding nationally with 2014 funds. In addition, as part of the training on new SP guidelines, a memo will be issued from the MOHSW reiterating that SP is provided free to the facility from the MSD.

PMI funding is supporting work to develop an integrated checklist for supportive supervision of all RCH services that could expand the existing general facility supervision checklist. Once developed, PMI plans to evaluate the feasibility of using this integrated checklist, as well as whether this results in improved supportive supervision. In addition, PMI will try to assess a reasonable schedule for conducting supervision visits given the length required for a complete supervision (one to three days depending on the size of the facility and number of services offered), as well as the number of people available for conducting supervision. It will need to be determined whether more extensive supervision provided at a lower frequency has the same, less, or more impact on health worker performance than the current quarterly supervision. Detailed supportive supervision conducted twice yearly may be more realistic and more useful to the sites.

Description and budget for proposed activities
PMI's funding for the following activities will contribute to a larger effort funded by other USAID health programs to improve demand for and the quality of antenatal care on the Mainland, including malaria prevention and treatment of acute infections.

Mainland
Policy and promotion including quarterly circular. Support ongoing efforts to obtain MOHSW approval for the change in IPTp policy and produce a quarterly bulletin to promote and inform health workers and others about malaria in pregnancy activities in Tanzania. *($100,000)*

Roll out of new guidelines. PMI will support implementation of the new IPTp guidelines at the health facility level throughout Mainland, including training and supervision of health workers. *($1,000,000)*

Safe Motherhood Campaign. Efforts will continue to ensure that ANC clients are counseled on the importance of IPTp, through co-investments in the safe motherhood campaign (*Wazazi Nipendeni*) supported by HIV, family planning, and MCH funds. PMI plans to expand this campaign by adding a component by which phone texts are sent to providers' cell phones to update them on new guidance related to IPTp. This will initially be rolled out in Lindi and Mtwara regions; and if found to augment efforts in increasing IPTp uptake it will be rolled out nationally. Money will be used to enhance communications in the community as well as in facilities to promote the up-take of IPTp 3+ as well as to promote attendance of ANC. BCC materials will be printed and disseminated systematically (targeting regions where IPTp up-take is low) this includes leaflets and other promotional materials in health facilities as well as media messages in the community. *($500,000)*

Supportive supervision in Lake Zone and Lindi and Mtwara Regions (coordinate with provider SMS pilot). PMI will provide funding for supportive supervision in these areas as a part of the effort to ensure proper implementation of the proposed new IPTp guidelines. *($600,000)*

Supply Chain Support PMI is working to address the problem of SP stock outs at ANC facilities. PMI will also support integration of SP into the national commodities electronic tracking and requisition system to ensure more consistent supplies of the drug, sulfadoxine-pyrimethamine, for IPTp at ANC clinics. The commodities partner will strengthen national and zonal commodity forecasting and distribution as well as facility based requisitions and reporting. ($200,000)

Technical assistance for MIP. CDC staff will provide technical support to implementation of new WHO IPT guidelines and strategies to improve IPT. *($12,100)*

Zanzibar

Evaluation of the adherence to the new guidelines. Technical assistance to develop and carry out evaluation of adherence to new guidelines to ensure that it provides a representative sample to reflect practices on both islands. ($100,000)

Supportive supervision. Support regular antenatal clinic supervisory visits by ministry staff, including ensuring adherence to the new policy (included in integrated supportive supervision budget).

Procurement of RDTs for use in the ANC (included in RDT budget).

4. CASE MANAGEMENT

DIAGNOSTICS

NMCP//ZMCP/PMI Objectives
Mainland

The goal of NMCP diagnostic strategy is to achieve universal access to high quality malaria diagnostic testing in both public and private health facilities. The current national 2013 targets for the 2008-2013 National Malaria Medium-Strategic Plan for case management are to increase to 80% the proportion of children under five years who: 1) receive appropriate treatment within 24 hours of onset of fever, and 2) receive appropriate management of both uncomplicated and severe malaria according to national treatment guidelines. In addition, the proportion of drug outlets selling antimalarial drugs according to the national treatment guideline should increase to 80%. A new Strategic Plan is under development.

In 2012, the NMCP changed its guidelines to state that all suspected malaria cases should be confirmed parasitologically prior to treatment. Microscopic examination of Giemsa-strained blood films remains a cornerstone of malaria diagnosis throughout Tanzania, but is only available at hospitals and some health centers; thus, most health centers use RDTs to confirm malaria cases.

Since 2006, PMI has supported the procurement and scale-up of RDTs, has assisted the MOHSW's Diagnostic Services Section to conduct comprehensive malaria diagnostics training sessions at the National Health Laboratory and Quality Assurance Training Center and has worked with WRAIR to develop a Malaria Reference Laboratory within the National Health Laboratory Quality Assurance and Training Centre (NHLQATC).

Unfortunately, several assessments have shown that the quality of both malaria microscopy and RDT testing is very poor at almost all levels of the health system. Currently, there is no system for laboratory quality assurance and quality control. In 2011-2012 PMI supported WRAIR to conduct a malaria diagnostics quality assurance evaluation and pilot program (see below).

NMCP is working with both the public and private sector to promote access for everyone to RDTs and ACTs. Current implementation strategies emphasize consolidating universal access to malaria diagnostics in both public and private health facilities, scale-up of diagnostics quality assurance, provision of appropriate management of uncomplicated malaria, and introduction of artesunate for treatment of severe malaria. NMCP's anticipated implementation strategies include scale up of mRDT provision in Accredited Drug Dispensing Outlet (ADDOs) and the social marketing of mRDT in ADDOs, both of which are being piloted with support from the Global Fund. NMCP received $17 million from Global Fund through 2015 to scale-up in the private sector. The scale-up also includes social marketing of RDTs in private for profit hospital and pharmacies. Since the Global Fund is supporting the NMCP in the private sector, PMI funds will be focused on the public sector.

Zanzibar
The Zanzibar malaria strategy also calls for parasitological confirmation for all patients with fever. Through PMI support, ZMCP has been able to provide RDTs to all 142 government health facilities and to enhance microscopy at hospitals and larger facilities. This has enabled the program to operate the well-functioning Malaria Early Epidemic Detection System (MEEDS). Malaria microscopy QA/QC was established in 2005 at 23 public health facilities in Zanzibar and as of 2012 had been expanded to 61 (38 public, 7 private, 4 faith-based organizations, 12 military). As in the Mainland, there is no established QA/QC for RDTs.

Progress over Past 12 Months
Mainland
The NMCP completed implementation of RDT provision to all government health facilities in all districts as of October 2012 and PMI procured 259,200 RDTs in support of this scale-up. PMI also supported an evaluation and quality assurance pilot program by the Walter Reed Army Institute of Research (WRAIR) across 16 hospital laboratories (microscopy) 48 representative health facilities that use RDTs.

Zanzibar
PMI supported the procurement of 212,500 RDTs for Zanzibar in 2012 and the expansion of RDT provision into the private sector. Global Fund will be covering the cost of all RDTs in Zanzibar for FY 2014.

Commodity Gap Analysis-Mainland

Product for Mainland	Quantity K/25	Status	Product Costs (USD)	Freight Costs (USD)	Total Costs (USD)
Malaria RDT K/25	840,426	Global Fund has committed all funding for this	$12,606,390	$1,890,959	$14,497,349

Challenges, opportunities, and threats

Evaluations have shown that overall malaria diagnostic testing performance is weak at all levels of the health system and that working conditions and RDT storage are generally unsatisfactory. PMI is providing technical and financial support to NMCP's efforts to develop and implement a nationally scalable approach to ensure high quality RDT results and a quality assurance/quality control (QA/QC) program for RDTs is nearing the final stages of development. Scale-up of this system will commence in Kagera Region in 2013 and be expanded to the remaining districts in 2014 and subsequent years. Complicating the expansion of this system is the very large number of health facilities in Tanzania (more than 5,000) and the limited supervisory capacity within the district and regional systems.

The Global Fund will provide the bulk of the RDTs needed for Mainland in 2014 thereby reducing the contribution needed from PMI. The Global Fund has recently revised and streamlined their procurement processes via Voluntary Pooled Procurement, which has significantly reduced, but not eliminated the risk of stockouts.

Plans and Justifications
Mainland

The new diagnostic policy emphasizes parasitological confirmation for all suspect malaria cases. This will mainly be accomplished through RDTs at peripheral levels, with microscopy at higher-level facilities. Reliance upon these methods for clinical decision making requires a robust QA system to monitor performance of both microscopy and RDTs. PMI funds will be used to support the development and implementation on the Mainland of a QA/QC system that focuses on RDTs rather than microscopy, as RDTs are the primary means of malaria diagnosis at lower-level health facilities where most patients seek care. The QA/QC system will be finalized in accordance with WHO guidelines and developed into a scalable package for national implementation. PMI's diagnostics partner will work with the necessary MOHSW units to develop an appropriate M&E strategy (including indicators) for the QA/QC program. A mechanism for supportive supervision for health care providers and laboratory technicians as well as follow-up of trained technicians serving the QA/QC plan at district and regional levels will be built into the program. Where possible, PMI will support the integration of malaria diagnostics training and QA/QC with HIV/AIDS and tuberculosis diagnosis through integrated planning and training.

The MOHSW is leading a new initiative to introduce a national integrated community health worker (CHW) program. At the moment there are many uncoordinated vertical programs working with CHWs, and CHWs in Tanzania do not currently perform mRDT testing and are not allowed to dispense ACTs.

The MOHSW has recognized the urgent need for an effective, coordinated, affordable and sustainable national CHW program. To date, there has been a stakeholders' meeting to explore sustainable ways for promoting community health in the country, a mapping exercise of current CHW initiatives, and there is a proposal for revision of the CHW policy guidelines. A task force was formed to develop a strategy. Some recommendations are:

1. To revise the existing Health Policy and Government Act to spell out the role of CHW at village level and prioritize the implementation of these policies;

2. To formalize the recruitment and remuneration of CHW;
3. To implement a reward system for CHWs;
4. To harmonize and standardize CHW roles and recognize them as formal health extension workers.

NMCP has requested PMI funds to help with gathering evidence-based data to inform the policy change and to support the addition of a malaria curative package (mRDT and ACT) at the CHW level.

Zanzibar

PMI will continue to support the implementation of a flexible system of external quality assurance to strengthen both RDT and microscopy performance and QA/QC at public facilities in Pemba and Unguja. This support will also be scaled up to private health facilities. PMI will support the establishment of a PCR laboratory that will be primarily used for entomologic and resistance monitoring but which could also perform other molecular studies including assessment of prevalence of asymptomatic infections and gametocytemia.

The ZMCP plans to use molecular biology techniques for epidemiologic and entomologic testing in Zanzibar. The ZMCP has personnel that are already trained in molecular assays, however at present all epidemiologic studies needed by the ZMCP have been carried out at laboratories of their collaborators. It has also outsourced some testing to the Public Health Laboratory/Ivo de Carnare Foundation (PHL/IDC) in Pemba; however due to costly overhead charges and the difficulties in obtaining the results, this is unsustainable. The ZMCP plans to look at sub-patent infections and is discussing future epidemiologic studies with collaborators (such as the Karolinska Institute) that will involve molecular biology assays. ZMCP plans to perform the molecular testing on site if the PCR capability is established. Similarly molecular testing for entomologic activities have in the past been outsourced (CDC, Liverpool School, IHI, etc.). This has resulted in slow turn around of data needed by the ZMCP and high costs due to overhead charges by some of the institutes.

The ZMCP will be able to sustain and maintain a PCR laboratory, since there will be no added personnel salary cost. Most of the cost will be for reagents and lab maintenance which the ZMCP can sustain in their budget and through collaborations. For entomologic activities it is estimated that the yearly running cost (reagents and disposable supplies) for processing entomologic samples, in-house, at the ZMCP will cost approximately $2,500 as compared to out-sourcing to IHI which currently costs about $4,500 - $5,000 annually.

Proposed Activities with FY 2014 Funding

Mainland

RDT Quality Assurance and Quality Control. Technical and programmatic support will be provided to the NMCP to support the scale-up of a QA/QC system beginning in one region (Kagera) with FY 2013 funds, but with the aim of extending to an additional 10 regions with FY 2014 funding. This will include support for refresher trainings as well as coordinated supportive supervision via Community, District, and Regional Health Management Teams. *($2,000,000)*

43

RDT procurement. PMI will continue to support forecasting, quantification, and procurement planning for RDTs. Although there have been no stock-outs in the past year, PMI will set aside funds to procure and distribute RDTs to health facilities via Medical Stores Department should they be required. If they are not required the funds will be reprogrammed to other PMI priority activities. *($1,000,000)*

RDT procurement for UNHCR. Currently, there are refugees in UNHCR camps in western Tanzania who do not have access to malaria laboratory diagnosis in MOHSW health facilities. With FY 2014 funding, PMI will procure and distribute RDT kits for UNHCR. *($50,000)*

Zanzibar
RDT procurement. PMI will procure RDTs for public health facilities in Zanzibar and scale-up RDT coverage to private sector hospitals and health facilities. In addition, these supplies may be used for active case detection and response in the event of an unusual increase in reported cases identified through the MEEDS. *($400,000)*

Mainland and Zanzibar
RDT and Microscopy Quality Assurance and Quality Control. This will include establishment of a reference slide bank, training of newly hired personnel, and supportive supervision of previously trained personnel in Zanzibar. To improve efficiency these funds will also support simultaneous development of the reference slide bank for the Mainland. *($104,000)*

Technical assistance. CDC will provide technical assistance on implementation of Quality Assurance and Quality Control Program. *($12,100)*

TREATMENT

NMCP/ZMCP/PMI Objectives
Mainland
ACTs were officially launched in Mainland Tanzania on December 15, 2006. The NMCP adopted artemether-lumefantrine (AL) as the first-line drug and artesunate-amodiaquine as the second-line drug for the treatment of uncomplicated malaria. The NMCP is currently revising the guidelines to change the regimen for treatment of severe malaria from quinine to injectable artesunate with parenteral quinine as an alternative where parenteral artesunate is not available.

The goal of NMCP malaria case management policy is to improve access and use of safe, effective, and affordable antimalarial drugs. The NMCP's priorities for FY 2014 are: to maintain and improve antimalarial drug supplies in the public sector; improve access, quality, and affordable ACTs in the private sector; strengthen the pharmacovigilance system; and strengthen therapeutic drug efficacy monitoring.

PMI has supported several interventions to improve access to ACTs and case management at the health facility level. Through the three Zonal Resource Centers of Arusha, Iringa, and Tabora PMI has supported the training of health workers in comprehensive malaria case management, including management of severe malaria and malaria in pregnancy.

Zanzibar

ACTs were deployed for the first time in Zanzibar in 2003 and the current first-line treatment for uncomplicated malaria is amodiaquine-artesunate. ACTs are widely available in health facilities. ACTs are extremely effective in clearing the asexual stages of malaria parasitemia but may not have an effect on the mature gametocytes which are necessary to complete the malaria life cycle in the mosquito vector. WHO recommends the use of single dose primaquine for all patients with confirmed *P. falciparum* infection in settings of low malaria transmission where elimination, as opposed to mere control, is the goal. Accordingly, the ZMCP plans to revise the case management guidelines to include primaquine on the first day of treatment with ACT. PMI is providing technical assistance to the ZMCP in forecasting, quantification, and procurement planning for ACTs and primaquine. ZMCP will follow the recommendations of the 2012 WHO Evidence Review Group on the safety and effectiveness of single dose primaquine as a *P. falciparum* gametocytocide. The recommendation states that when G6PD testing is not available, a single dose of 0.25 mg base/kg primaquine in addition to ACT on day 0 should be given to all patients with falciparum malaria with the exception of pregnant women and infants less than one year of age.

Progress over Past 12 Months
Mainland

PMI provided technical assistance for the annual quantification and procurement planning for ACTs and RDTs, including procurement planning for commodities funded by the Global Fund. Bi-annual reviews were done to update stock tables and procurement plans. This exercise has assisted the Ministry of Health & Social Welfare (MOHSW), NMCP, Medical Stores Department (MSD), and the Pharmaceutical Services Section to manage the commodity pipeline for the country. The MOHSW has set minimum and maximum standards for stock availability at six and nine months, respectively.

PMI has continued to provide technical assistance and funding to NMCP to update the National Diagnostic and Treatment Guidelines and to plan for countrywide roll-out. The revised guidelines will be submitted to the MOHSW and dissemination to all public hospitals and health centers will be done in June/July 2013; dissemination to all dispensaries will be done in October 2013.

Zanzibar

PMI, through its implementing partner, has continued to support the procurement of ACTs for government facilities. The system has worked well; stockouts rates of ACT declined from 20% in May 2012 to 8% in December 2012.

PMI has supported the strengthening of logistics system for ordering essential medicines, which includes ACT and mRDTs (ZILS). Two hundred and thirty-three health workers from 86 health facilities and 43 central medical stores (CMS) and districts management team staff have received training on ordering and stock management. The project is also working to improve the distribution system for essential medicines. A team of technical advisors are working to re-define the distribution route using Llamasoft software. This will improve CMS efficiency in distribution thus reducing operation costs. On an annual basis, with support from partners, the ZMCP and

CMS staff conduct quantification of malaria commodities and support monitoring the supply plan for the whole country.

Commodity Gap Analysis
Funding for ACTs in the public sector has been supported primarily by Global Fund and PMI. Because of Tanzania's successful Global Fund grants, PMI currently provides only gap funding support for malaria commodities.

PROJECTED COUNTRY ACT NEEDS			
	2013	2014	2015
6 X 1 20/120mg FDC	6,279,810	4,151,460	2,477,460
6 X 2 20/120mg FDC	5,097,120	2,833,830	2,109,690
6 X 3 20/120mg FDC	4,501,470	1,659,240	1,805,220
6 X 4 20/120mg FDC	8,102,550	4,090,650	3,024,510
TOTAL	23,980,950	12,735,180	9,416,880

Zanzibar
The Global Fund will be procuring all the ACT needs for Zanzibar, thus no PMI funds are being budgeted for medication.

Plans and Justifications
PMI will support NMCP and the Zonal Resource Centres to roll out the revised NMCP Diagnostic and Treatment Guidelines to private facilities. This will include development of standard operating procedures for management of severe malaria and malaria in pregnancy, as well as the training of health workers at the dispensary level in comprehensive malaria case management. Tanzania has enough support from Global Fund to procure ACTs for the public sector. However, because of the possibility of delays, PMI has allocated FY 2014 funds to provide an emergency stock of approximately 2 million ACT treatments (average cost of $1 per treatment). In the event that these funds are not needed, they will be reallocated to other priority PMI gaps.

Programmatic decisions regarding changes to malaria treatment policy require continuous data to demonstrate that first and second-line regimens remain effective at treating malaria parasitemia. Until molecular markers of resistance are identified, measurement and reporting of parasite clearance on day 3 after treatment with ACTs is particularly important, as this is one of the first signals of artemisinin resistance available today. PMI will support drug efficacy monitoring following the standards WHO protocol at four to five sentinel sites on the Mainland.

To improve the procurement of needed commodities, PMI will support forecasting, quantification, and procurement planning for ACTs and RDTs and will support the MSD and

MOHSW Pharmaceutical Supply Unit to institutionalize supply chain management functions. Support for malaria commodity logistics will continue to focus on monitoring the Integrated Logistics System to ensure continued availability of ACTs and other malarial commodities at health facility level. The logistics monitoring capacity of the district malaria/IMCI focal people will be strengthened and additional support provided on inventory control procedures at central, regional, and facility levels.

Pharmaceutical and supply chain strengthening activities will also include: conducting quarterly end use verification surveys to a sample of health facilities and zonal warehouses to monitor the availability of key antimalarial commodities; visits to health facilities and regional warehouses to detect and respond to critical issues such as ACT (or other drug) stockouts; establishing systems for monitoring distribution of ACTs and RDTs from the Medical Store departments to health facilities; and repacking of ACTs. PMI support will address medical waste management and final disposal, as per U.S. Government and local environmental laws.

Currently, ACTs are packaged in boxes which contain 25 (on Zanzibar) and 30 (on Mainland) treatment courses. In low transmission areas both on Mainland and particularly in Zanzibar, this results in substantial over-stocking of ACTs, particularly as it is necessary to stock at least one of each box of each of four different doses. Funds will be provided to MSD to allow the individual dosing cards to be re-packaged such that facilities can be sent lots of five treatment courses. No changes will be made to the packaging of the actual dosage cards. This is anticipated to save funds and reduce waste of ACTs which might otherwise expire unused on shelves. To ensure the integrity of the product, this would be done by pharmacists at Central Medical Stores so that facilities can be supplied with the appropriate number and types of doses.

Diagnosis and Management of Febrile Illness
PMI will continue to contribute to the integrated service delivery project in the Lake Zone aimed at improving child health through strengthening the capacity of facility-based health workers to provide fundamental diagnostic and treatment services for malaria and other major causes of severe febrile illness and death in children under five. Lake Zone is one of the most populous of the eight zones making up Mainland Tanzania with a total population of 6.3 million. At the same time, community-focused efforts with funding from Maternal and Child Health and HIV/AIDS is contributing to reductions in under-five mortality by strengthening the referral of sick children identified in the community; this is part of PMI and joint USAID programming in child health.

PMI will support the training of health care workers in 57 health care facilities in case management. It will also train laboratory workers on RDT and quality malaria microscopy, and develop a system for checking accuracy. The team will continue training the Regional and Community Health Management Teams in supportive supervision and onsite mentoring to facility-based quality improvement teams, and will arrange for monthly visits from coaches. These interventions will upgrade the skills of health workers in quality improvement and case management of febrile illness. The program will ensure availability of updated guidelines and algorithms for health facilities to aid in differential diagnosis for febrile illnesses. PMI will also facilitate linkages between the primary health facilities and the community health workers.

In order to increase locally-raised resources to support case management, PMI will facilitate identification of private sector organizations to support child health and management of malaria and febrile illness as part of their corporate social responsibility. The private sector organizations include private corporate companies like the mining companies in the Lake Zone and banking companies. PMI will support Council Health Management Teams to leverage funds from these companies to support the availability of commodities like mRDTs and ACTs in their respective councils. Community networks and leaders will be organized and trained to promote health-seeking behaviors and address obstacles to accessing services. These partnerships and networks will strengthen referral systems and improve access for the most vulnerable children.

Zanzibar
PMI will support ZMCP to collect consumption and logistics data needed for annual quantification and procurement planning, implement end use verification surveys to monitor availability and use of malaria commodities at health facility level, and handle medical waste and final disposal of expired ACTs and RDTs. PMI will support the revision and dissemination of the ZMCP treatment guidelines. These are expected to include the addition of primaquine treatment of all confirmed cases to reduce gametocytemia and also the discontinuation of intermittent treatment of pregnant women with SP.

Proposed Activities with FY 2014 Funding

Mainland
Management of Febrile Illness. Continue to contribute to the integrated service delivery project in the Lake Zone aimed at improving child health through strengthening the capacity of facility-based health workers to provide fundamental diagnostic and treatment services for malaria and other major causes of severe febrile illness. *($750,000)*

ACT Procurement to fill Emergency Needs in the Public Sector. The Global Fund is expected to procure all ACT needs on the Mainland. However, experience has shown that PMI has had to procure emergency stock on numerous occasions due to delayed disbursement GF money. Thus, PMI is planning an emergency fund to procure ACTs to ensure no stockouts. In the event these funds are not needed the money will be reprogrammed for other PMI priority needs. *($2,000,000)*

ACT Procurement for UNHCR. Currently, there are refugees in UNHCR camps in western Tanzania who do not have access to ACTs or RDTs through MOHSW health facilities. PMI will procure and distribute ACTs treatments and RDTs for UNHCR. *($50,000)*

Integrated Community Case Management (iCCM). PMI funds will be used to support stakeholder consultation meetings, the formation of a national CHW policy, and support the inclusion of a malaria curative package at the CHW level as well as printing and dissemination of guidelines. ($100,000)

Strengthen Pharmaceutical Management and Supply Chain System. PMI will support improved quantification for RDTs and antimalarial drugs, transportation, storage and record keeping. ($750,000)

Roll-out of Revised Treatment Guidelines. This will include preparation and dissemination of national guidelines, preparation and production of a training package and BCC material, dissemination of the training package through cascade trainings, refresher training support, and supply and instruction on artesunate use. ($1,000,000)

Routine therapeutic drug efficacy monitoring. PMI funds will be used to support routine in vivo efficacy monitoring of after artemether-lumefantrine treatment at four to five sites. *($250,000)*

Zanzibar
Procurement of Primaquine. Procure primaquine for new malaria treatment policy. ($1,000)

Repackaging of ACTs. Current packaging of ACT meds bundles together multiple doses of medication resulting in wastage. PMI funds will be used to support repackaging of medications into smaller unit to reduce waste. ($100,000)

Strengthen Pharmaceutical Management and Supply Chain System. PMI will support improved quantification for RDTs and antimalarial drugs, transportation, storage and record keeping. *($250,000)*

Updating Case Management Guidelines PMI will support the revision and dissemination of the ZMCP treatment guidelines, which are expected to include the addition of primaquine treatment of all confirmed cases to reduce gametocytemia and also the discontinuation of intermittent treatment of pregnant women with SP. *($50,000)*

5. MONITORING AND EVALUATION

NMCP/ZMCP/PMI Objectives

Epidemic Surveillance & Response
Mainland
True malaria epidemics are uncommon on the Mainland, but seasonal increases in transmission do occur. Thus, the Mainland is working towards developing a sustainable early epidemic detection system that can detect sudden increases in transmission. NMCP principal objectives for epidemic surveillance are: 1) to attain 100% reporting of routine and periodic key malaria indicators from all districts, 2) to strengthen malaria surveillance to detect 100% of malaria epidemics within one week of onset, 3) to effectively manage malaria epidemics within two weeks of detection, and 4) to strengthen monitoring and evaluation of malaria control interventions, activities, policies and strategies.

Zanzibar
PMI continues to focus epidemic surveillance and response activities in Zanzibar which is in the pre-elimination stage. In FY 2008, PMI provided technical and financial support to ZMCP to develop and implement a Malaria Early Epidemic Detection System (MEEDS). The system includes a strategy to collect daily data for three key indicators (total visits, confirmed malaria positive, confirmed malaria negative) among outpatients visiting peripheral health facilities.

Weekly aggregated data, stratified by age, are transmitted from each health facility using a customized cell phone menu. All data are received by a computer server operated by a Tanzanian telecommunications company. The weekly data are processed by the server and packaged into two useful formats: 1) text messages with weekly data summaries sent to cell phones of key ZMCP staff and district medical officers; and 2) longitudinal weekly data made available for viewing over a secure web site.

Zanzibar instituted a Malaria Case Notification system at the end of 2011 with the aim of investigating every confirmed case of malaria infection within 24 hours of notification from the health facility. In this system the District Malaria Surveillance Officer travels to the case household to interview and test household members as well as those of neighboring households.

Monitoring and Evaluation (M&E)
Mainland
The NMCP's objectives for M&E in addition to the above epidemic surveillance objectives are: 1) to attain 100% reporting of routine and periodic key malaria indicators from all districts, and 2) to strengthen monitoring and evaluation of malaria control interventions, activities, policies and strategies.

Mainland and Zanzibar
The NMCP receives a large amount of data from its own M&E activities and those of multiple national and international malaria partners. For several years, PMI has been supporting efforts to: 1) strengthen the data management unit within the NMCP to store, analyze, and disseminate information for decision making, 2) hold regular meeting to discuss M&E activities, and 3) make regular M&E supervisory visits to the field. PMI will continue to support these activities.

PMI has worked closely with colleagues from NMCP, ZMCP, Global Fund, WHO, World Bank, Malaria Control and Evaluation Partnership in Africa, other units of the MOHSW (e.g., HMIS, Integrated Disease Surveillance and Response (IDSR) , and Health Sector Reform), and other sectors of the Government of Tanzania (National Bureau of Statistics, Ministry of Education) to promote coordinated M&E efforts.

The following data sources and timelines provide the foundation for PMI's and the Government of Tanzania's evaluation of malaria control outcomes and impact.

Demographic and Health Surveys (DHS). Every four to five years, the DHS collects nationally representative, population-based data for a wide variety of demographic and health indicators, including core malaria intervention coverage indicators, anemia, and all-cause, under-five child mortality. It is conducted by National Bureau of Statistics with technical assistance from Macro International. The last DHS was conducted in Tanzania during December 2009 – May 2010. The next Tanzania DHS is scheduled for 2014-2015.

Malaria Indicator Survey (MIS). The MIS survey assesses core household coverage and morbidity indicators used in Tanzania. The most recent MIS (combined with an AIDS Indicator Survey) was conducted in 2011-12 with funding from both PMI and PEPFAR (see _Progress on Coverage and Impact Indicators section_ for results). The main benefit to malaria is that with the larger AIS funding and sample size, regional level data are obtained for parasitemia (as with HIV prevalence) without an added cost.

Service Provision Assessment (SPA). The Service Provision Assessment is an evaluation conducted every four to five years in public and private health facilities and collects actionable information on the availability and quality of facility infrastructure, resources, and management system and on services, including child health, maternal health, and infectious diseases such as malaria, tuberculosis, and HIV. Tanzania carried out a SPA in 2006 that included a malaria case management module that provided baseline information for PMI. A SPA is planned with FY 2012 PMI funding.

Health Management Information System (HMIS). The objectives of the HMIS are to provide data for monitoring key impact indicators over time: 1) standardized laboratory-confirmed malaria cumulative incidence per year, among patients under five years old, patients older than five years, and pregnant women; 2) IPTp uptake among pregnant women; and 3) standardized crude laboratory-confirmed malaria death rate among patients under five years, patients older than five years, and pregnant women. Historically, the majority of malaria cases reported to this system represented clinical diagnoses, usually non-specific fever. However, this situation is changing as Tanzania continues to scale up the use of RDTs at health facilities of all levels. HMIS information is reported annually through Council Health Management Teams and the Health Statistics Abstract. Data flows from the health facility level up to the central level, where it is compiled, analyzed, and reported. Currently, a major multi-donor initiative (including PEPFAR) is underway to reform the existing HMIS platform. Multiple donors have committed more than $5 million to strengthen the system and an operational plan has been developed. PMI staff continue to ensure that malaria is well represented in the ongoing implementation plans for HMIS reform.

Integrated Disease Surveillance and Response (IDSR). IDSR captures notifiable/epidemic prone diseases and are reported on daily, weekly or monthly basis depending on the disease. New malaria variables – number (suspect cases) tested, number positive and clinical cases – have been added to the IDSR form. The long term strategy for IDSR is to use mobile phone technology for data submission (eIDSR). When eIDSR is implemented, it will use DHIS2 as the platform for data capture, analysis and reporting. This will reduce the duplicate facility level data collection, reporting and entry.

Implementing Partner Reporting System (IPRS). Effective performance monitoring is critical to PMI success in achieving results. Since 2010, PMI has relied on the Implementing Partner Reporting System (IPRS) as the source of data for Annual Reporting. IPRS is a web based system where PMI implementing Partners enter their performance data on quarterly basis. This contract is ending December 2013.

Monitoring and Evaluation Strengthening Initiative (MESI). This is an on-going activity, led by the Government of Tanzania and supported partially by PMI, aimed at instituting enhanced surveillance measures in the Lake Zone.

Entomologic monitoring
Mainland

The national resistance monitoring on the Mainland, initiated in 2008, is currently supported by PMI through its implementing partner NIMR. In 2012, with evidence of increasing insecticide resistance, resistance surveillance was increased from 14 to 26 sentinel sites from 22 regions in the Mainland, to include the PMI IRS districts of Kagera, Muelba and Mara. These sites were selected based on areas with high malaria prevalence, history of insecticide use (both for public health and in agriculture) in the area, level of ITN coverage, demography (urban/rural) and site accessibility.

The NIMR-Mwanza entomology facility, serving as a regional entomology center for the Lake Victoria basin, conducts routine entomologic monitoring of IRS activities in the districts, Chato, Karagwe, Muleba, and Mara. Working with the Regional/District Health authorities, monthly mosquito collections are sent to NIMR-Mwanza for processing and analysis. In addition, cone wall bioassays are conducted to monitor residual insecticide activity for IRS at Kagera, Mwanza and Mara.

With rapid scale-up of ITNs and IRS, entomologic evaluations are showing a trend towards residual malaria transmission from indoor to out-door biting mosquitoes. This could compromise the effectiveness of the ITNs and IRS and may indicate the need for increased entomologic surveillance and a timely reporting of data.

Through a partnership between NIMR, IHI, London School of Hygiene and Tropical Medicine, and the Kilimanjaro Christian Medical College, PMI is supporting an assessment in Muleba of whether ITNs can sustain the transmission reduction gains made by IRS following the withdrawal of IRS in an area with high ITN coverage using a two-arm cluster-randomized design. Two districts were selected. In year one (2011), both arms received both IRS and ITN. In the second year (2012), one arm will continue to receive IRS and ITNs while the other arm would receive ITNs alone. The study is now complete and results will be disseminated end 2013.

Zanzibar
The ZMCP conducted wall contact bioassays to monitor the efficacy of the insecticide on sprayed surfaces, using their colony of susceptible *An. gambiae s.s.* The ZMCP continues to conduct yearly insecticide resistance monitoring in both islands and routine entomological monitoring at seven sentinel sites, four sites on Unguja and three on Pemba. This provides information on vector species and density, human blood feeding index and malaria infection rates in the various vector species. In addition, ZMCP has implemented in-depth entomologic assessments of "hot spots" identified from the MEEDS data. This is complemented with spot-check investigations from randomly selected sites based on weekly MEEDs reporting.

Progress over Past 12 Months

Mainland
<u>Epidemic response.</u> The NMCP has begun the planning process for implementation of a MEEDS system on the Mainland in three districts of the Lake Zone.

Entomologic Monitoring. There are currently 26 sentinel sites for the national insecticide resistance monitoring program and yearly insecticide resistance monitoring is carried out at 14 of these sites, using the WHO standard assay for permethrin, bendiocarb, fenitrothion, lambdacyhalothrin and DDT. Between June and December 2012, insecticide resistance monitoring was conducted at the 12 new sentinel sites and 2 old sites of Moshi and Arumeru where insecticide resistance has been previously reported.

Currently entomologic monitoring for vector species is being carried out regularly at seven sentinel sites. In 2012, combination of light traps, pyrethrum spray catches, and pit traps are used. PCR species identification showed that vector species composition varied between regions.

Monitoring of the residual efficacy of the IRS in the Lake Zone was conducted from June 2011 – March 2012. A total of seven rounds of WHO cone bioassays were conducted, at monthly intervals, at the three sentinel sites in the Kagera region where bendiocarb (a carbamate) had been used for the seventh round of IRS. Similar cone bioassays were carried out Mwanza and Mara regions where lambdacyhalothrin had been used. A total of four sentinel sites were tested, two in each region. The cone bioassays using susceptible _An. gambiae s.s_, from the NIMR-Mwanza facility were tested on different wall surfaces (mud, cement, painted/whitewash, and wood). Painted/whitewashed surfaces had longer residual efficacy of six months post-spray for lambdacyhalothrin and four to five months for bendiocarb treated surfaces. On mud surfaces the residual effect of bendiocarb and lambdacyhalothrin declined more rapidly than on the other surfaces.

The IHI/NIMR pilot of community-based entomologic monitoring system has been scaled-up to 14 sites using the Ifakara tent traps, with some sites located in PMI IRS areas. In general there are low numbers of mosquitoes being collected in all the sites, with Moshi having the highest density. From July – September 2012, 75% of 403 mosquitoes collected were _An. gambiae s.l_ and the final analysis is being carried out. The mobile phone real-time submission of the data has been set up and piloted with the mosquito data collected.

Zanzibar
Epidemic response. The MEEDS system covers a total of 142 reporting sites, or all government health facilities in Zanzibar and expansion has started to some private health facilities. A data quality assessment showed that the completeness of reporting has reached 100% with 80% reporting within one week. There is 95% agreement between MEEDS and HMIS data.

Between September 2012 and April 2013, 463 (73% of total MEEDS cases) were investigated through the Malaria Case Notification system. A total of 2,769 household members were tested of whom 162 (6%) were positive. Fifty-five percent of the cases reported no recent travel, indicating that transmission occurred locally. The overall functioning of the MCN is good; a recent assessment showed that 82% of cases were followed up by the DMSO within 24 hours. Nevertheless, some impediments to timely and complete follow-up remain.

ZMCP also conducted active case detection (ACD) in several _shehias_ (Tundaua, Rehekani, Kinowe, Chimba and Finya) where MEEDS data had indicated an upswing in cases. A total of

9,008 asymptomatic people were tested of which 37 (0.4%) were found to be parasitemic and treated. Although the ZMCP has pushed strongly for wide-spread ACD over the past two to three years, it is very labor intensive and has a low yield. In contrast, ACD among family members of documented cases yields more cases. The ZMCP is revising their epidemic response guidelines to focus future ACD efforts on family/household members. The new ACD strategy will be reflected in their Strategic Plan.

Entomologic monitoring. WHO insecticide resistance testing for deltamethrin, permethrin, bendiocarb, and DDT was carried out in 2012 with mosquitoes collected from four sites in Unguja and three sites in Pemba. In addition, lambdacyhalothrin testing was carried out at Unguja. The IRS and ITN program in Zanzibar has reduced the mosquito populations in both islands such it was only possible to perform testing of all four insecticides on mosquitoes collected from Uwadani, Pemba. With the current trend of resistance seen in pyrethroids (deltamethrin and permethrin) in both Pemba and Unjuga, it is critical to intensify monitoring of pyrethroids and the possible impact of resistance on the ITN program.

Routine entomologic monitoring continues at four sentinel sites in Unguja and three in Pemba. After initial morphological identification of the mosquito collections (from pit traps, pyrethrum spray catches, light traps, and man landing collections), the material is then tested for malaria infection using the ELISA method at the Unguja entomology laboratory. The PCR species identification is currently being carried out at IHI since there is no PCR capability in Zanzibar. Vector density distribution in Zanzibar is bi-modal, associated with the two rainy seasons.

There has been a shift in vector species composition and vector dynamics on both islands since 2005. *An. arabiensis* is now the predominant vector in both Pemba and Unguja. *An. merus* (22%) was also found in Pemba. Man landing collections at the sentinel sites continue to show that transmission is occurring mainly through outdoor biting, a pattern consistent with the predominance of the more exophilic and exophagic *An. arabiensis*.

Monitoring and Evaluation
In 2007 and 2011, PMI co-funded the first and second population-based THMIS. The 2011-12 THMIS survey results were officially released in March 2013. Zonal disseminations are underway and the PMI team provided comments on both dissemination materials and products, such as Malaria Atlas. The final report has provided critical data for NMCP/PMI's effort to evaluate the impact of malaria control efforts. With FY 2012 funds, PMI contributed $450,000 to support the second national facility based survey—the Tanzania Service Provision Assessment (TSPA). The TSPA will be implemented in May 2013 and will provide information at regional level on availability, readiness, and quality of malaria and other health and HIV/AIDS services; it is currently in the planning stages. Stakeholder meetings have been conducted on Mainland and Zanzibar, and included key stakeholders. PMI has supported the integration of malaria indicators into the electronic IDSR surveillance system. This system has conducted personnel training and been piloted in the Lake Zone, but is still not operational, thus necessitating continued reliance on paper-based reporting. A PMI technical team visited in March 2013 and will develop a concept note to guide the piloting of the recommended actions for strengthening the routine surveillance system.

The malaria program review (MPR) is a periodic joint management process for assessing progress and performance of the national malaria control program with the aim of improving performance and refining or redefining the strategic direction and focus.

In 2011, the NMCP, in collaboration with partners, undertook a comprehensive review of the progress and performance of the malaria program for the period of 2002 to 2011. The objective of the review was to assess the current policies, strategies, and activities with a view of strengthening the malaria control program and health systems used in delivery of malaria control services. The major MPR finding was a significant increase in resources for malaria that led to scale up of malaria control interventions, especially ITNs and ACTs in both the public and private sector. The MPR identified gaps in the management capacity at NMCP, lack of government of Tanzania capacity to sustain the gains, absence of a robust ITN strategy to sustain net availability, inadequate use of new epidemiological data to target interventions, an outdated insecticide resistance mitigation plan that is threatening the IRS and ITN strategy, and lack of innovations to improve antenatal attendance and IPTp coverage. Most of the identified gaps are now being addressed by the NMCP.

Challenges, opportunities, and threats
The Tanzania Impact Evaluation has highlighted the poor quality of malaria data collected through HMIS. Moreover, the private sector does not participate in the HMIS. Reported malaria case numbers are frequently based on clinical case definition (non-laboratory confirmed), summary forms are incomplete and submitted either late or frequently not at all. Anecdotal evidence indicates that reporting rate from facilities is less than 50%. In addition, NMCP seems to have recurrent problems with access and availability of data from established databases, such as the HMIS and IDSR. Full implementation of the electronic IDSR, intended to be a cornerstone of malaria surveillance, has experienced numerous and lengthy delays. In addition, the NMCP is understaffed and lacks capacity to effectively use data.

Plans and Justification
Mainland
For the past two years, the PMI team has given financial support to help establish an electronic IDSR system but it has not resulted in a functioning system. Because the eIDSR system is not yet operational, the NMCP currently relies on the HMIS system as well as the SPD to monitor malaria cases and other indicators. During the interim period before the electronic IDSR system becomes fully functional PMI will also support the strengthening of the paper-based reporting system.

PMI has identified Tanzania for the pilot routine information system strengthening activity. This selection was based on the findings from Tanzania malaria control impact evaluation (completed 2012) which noted that the poor quality of malaria data (appropriate case definition, completeness, and timeliness of reports) from the routine system made it difficult to analyze and interpret the data. The aim of routine information system strengthening activity is to improve the quality of malaria data available from the HMIS. The focus in Tanzania will be sub-national in scope, and collaborative with other partners and stakeholders in prioritization of data gaps and activities to address these gaps.

PMI will support the planned Mission-wide M&E services contract which will cover a broader range of M&E services such as: 1) performance monitoring (via a web-based reporting system), 2) M&E Capacity Building and GIS mapping of USAID/Tanzania activities, and 3) Data Quality Assessment and Evaluation. The web-based performance monitoring system will collect and store data before reporting and includes all required PMI reporting indicators. Implementing partners enter performance data quarterly and upload their narrative reports that serve as data sources.

M&E capacity building will be provided to implementing partners, in particular to develop activity M&E plans and other M&E functions necessary for performance management. These include target setting and conducting baseline surveys. Realizing the potential of GIS in decision making, the Mission will also map all activities including malaria interventions. To ensure that high quality data are reported, the M&E contractor will conduct data quality assessments.

Zanzibar

PMI will support maintenance of MEEDS at all 142 government health facilities and eventual scale up to 100% of private facilities. Refresher training and supportive supervision visits for diagnostics and surveillance will be increased. PMI will continue to support active case detection among household and neighborhood contacts of confirmed cases. Epidemic confirmation procedures will be maintained and response systems further strengthened to allow ZMCP to deploy a small cadre of trained staff to investigate all suspected epidemics.

Proposed Activities with FY 2014 Funding

Mainland

Paper-Based Reporting. PMI will support a paper-based reporting system in the Lake Zone until such time as the electronic IDSR system becomes fully functional. *($500,000)*

Integrated Supportive Supervision. The NMCP receives reports and data from a wide array of their own M&E activities, plus ongoing activities in other parts of the MOHSW, sentinel surveillance sites, and from all PMI-funded partners. PMI support will strengthen the data management unit within NMCP to collect, store, analyze, display, and disseminate information for decision making. Support will also enable NMCP staff to complete supervision visits every other month, including per diem and vehicle expenses. PMI will support the development of integrated supportive supervision that will coordinate NMCP supervisory activities both across malaria interventions and with other non-malaria activities. Districts and health facilities for supervision will be prioritized based on agreed criteria and will include monitoring of malaria prevention activities in the communities like IRS and TNVS. Supervisors will use checklists to record their findings, and incorporate data into quarterly HMIS reports and presentations for NMCP and partners. *($500,000)*

Malaria Program Review. PMI in partnership with other partners will contribute towards the next MPR on Mainland. The MPR will assess the progress made in addressing the gaps identified in the 2011 MPR, and the innovations made to reduce further malaria transmission on Mainland. ($25,000)

Technical Support for Mission monitoring and evaluation. PMI will contribute proportionally to the planned Mission-wide M&E services contract which covers a broader range of M&E services within the Health Office including performance monitoring of PMI indicators. *($390,000)*

External End of Project Evaluations of URC and JHU-TCCP.
PMI will co-fund with other USAID health programs the midterm and end of project evaluations of the management of febrile illnesses project (Tibu Homa) in Lake Zone and the Tanzania Capacity and Communication Project a Behavior Change communication program. These evaluations will assess project performance and look at whether these projects achieved results. These findings will inform future programmatic planning. *($125,000)*

Entomologic monitoring. This includes entomologic monitoring in the Lake Region, insecticide resistance monitoring at the national sentinel sites and will include in the Lake Victoria Basin area, materials for WHO bioassays to monitor both IRS and ITNs. PMI will continue to support insecticide resistance and bioassays at 26 national sites to monitor national ITN and IRS interventions. This will provide a database of insecticide resistance and efficacy for the NMCP and other partners. *($650,000)*

Molecular biology support. PMI will provide funds for establishment of a PCR laboratory and procurement of supplies. *($94,000)*

Zanzibar
Maintain MEEDS and Outbreak Preparedness/Response. Support readiness for malaria epidemic investigation and response (e.g., active case detection using RDTs, mass treatment of fever cases in the affected community, focal IRS, and supplies for management of severe malaria) will require adequate stocks and periodic rotation of commodities. *($550,000)*

Integrated Supportive Supervision. PMI will continue to fund integrated laboratory and MEEDS surveillance supportive supervision visits on a quarterly basis at all government health facilities throughout Pemba and Unguja as well as scale-up to private facilities. This type of integrated visit to the health facilities helps ensure diagnostics and surveillance systems are harmonized. Analysis of the support supervision visits data will be performed on a semi-annual basis and used for further refining and strengthening Zanzibar diagnostics and MEEDS systems. *($40,000)*

Entomologic monitoring. PMI will continue support to ZMCP in entomologic monitoring in view emerging pyrethroid resistance in Zanzibar, changes in insecticide class for IRS activities, shift from blanket spraying to targeted and focal IRS strategies and scale-up to universal ITN coverage. The program will continue to review and re-focus the current entomology surveillance strategies in line with the changes in vector control strategies. Investigation into malaria "hot-spot" areas is crucial to Zanzibar's strategy for malaria elimination. PMI will continue to assist the ZMCP in developing vector control guidelines for the malaria early warning system. *($160,000)*

Procurement of Entomological Reagents. PMI will continue to support procurement of entomology supplies and laboratory reagents for the insectary, testing mosquitoes for malaria parasites, and for insecticide resistance testing. Laboratory testing will include molecular biology, immunological and biochemical methods. *($10,000)*

Mainland and Zanzibar

Technical assistance for M&E. CDC staff will conduct two TA visit to assist with strengthening of malaria surveillance and other monitoring activities, including technical expertise in malaria program reviews, national and special surveys, and routine health information systems. *($24,200)*

Technical assistance for entomological monitoring. CDC staff will conduct two TA visit to support entomological monitoring for Mainland and Zanzibar. To provide technical assistance to NIMR Mwanza to achieve the necessary routine entomologic monitoring of post spray activities and to monitor the entomology effects of the U5CC and the UCC in non-IRS area. In Zanzibar CDC will provide technical assistance to increase ELISA capability to include blood meal analysis for vector biting preferences and essays for mosquitoes. This activity includes technical support for entomological supplies because the reagents have been difficult to obtain locally. *($24,200)*

Technical assistance for PCR. CDC staff will conduct one TA visit to assist with capacity building and implementation of a molecular laboratory to conduct epidemiologic and entomologic monitoring in Zanzibar. *($12,100)*

M&E Table

Data Source	2011	2012	2013	2014	2015	2016
Household Surveys	THMIS co-funded with PEPFAR (Findings disseminated) Data sets available			DHS (Planned)		
Other Surveys		SARA (Funded by GF) Report and data set available	TSPA(Preparations underway) PMI team provided comments on survey instrument			
Malaria Surveillance and routine system support	MEEDS (Zanzibar)	MEEDS (Zanzibar)	IDSR (Pilot in Lake Zone)	IDSR		
Other Data Sources						

Operational Research

NCMP/ZNMP/PMI objectives

While PMI supports operational research to help guide malaria control activities, neither the NMCP nor ZMCP has an official OR strategy.

Progress in last 12 months

Mainland

Monitoring Parasitemia Prevalence among Pregnant Women and Infants. This operations research (OR) activity was funded in the 2011 MOP and is currently underway. It explores the operational feasibility of screening: 1) all pregnant women at time of first antenatal care visit and 2) all infants at the time of measles immunization (approximately 9 months of age) for malaria using RDTs. Data is captured and a summary sent at monthly intervals using a simple text message system that does not require special phones or cost to the health facility. This approach has been implemented at 54 RCH sites in Kagera, Mwanza, and Mara Regions from December 2012 and March 2013. A total of 18,911 pregnant women attended first ANC and 6,926 infants attended measles vaccination, with 52.9% and 72.6% tested with mRDT, respectively. The overall prevalence of malaria parasitaemia among pregnant women and infants was 12.2% (95%

confidence interval [CI] 11.5-12.8) and 10.1% (95% CI 9.3-11.0), respectively. This is felt to be a useful way to monitor parasitemia prevalence longitudinally, and thought is being given to scaling this up as part of routine monitoring in Lake Zone.

Zanzibar
Placental parasitemia study
Placental parasitemia among women who have not had intermittent preventive treatment (IPTp) for malaria in Zanzibar. The goal of this study was to measure placental parasitemia rates among pregnant women delivering in the selected facilities in Zanzibar who have not received IPTp and to provide cost-benefit analyses to help inform policy decisions on the IPTp program in Zanzibar. This OR activity was funded in 2011. A total of 1,356 women were enrolled in the study from August 2011 – September 2012. Nine had active placental malaria infection as determined by polymerase chain reaction of placental blood, representing an infection rate of 0.6%. One of the women with placental malaria, of unknown HIV status, delivered a stillborn infant; none of the other cases of active infection were associated with poor birth outcomes. The costing component of this study is on-going; a report has been completed and a paper is being drafted for publication.

Proposed Activities with FY 2014 Funding
Mainland
Monitoring SP Resistance and Effectiveness
In October 2012, WHO released an updated recommendation that IPTp-SP should be provided to all pregnant women at each ANC visit after the completion of the first[t] trimester, provided that there are four weeks between doses. Tanzania is changing its guidance to reflect the new WHO guidance; it is hoped that this will improve uptake of IPTp2. However, given the potential risks associated with use of IPTp-SP in areas with highly resistant parasites, monitoring for the development of these resistant parasites is crucial. PMI will monitor the prevalence of resistance markers against SP in parasites recovered from pregnant women attending first ANC visits. We will also monitor the birth weight and number of SP doses of women delivering at the same facilities. The data collected over time, will tell us if SP is losing its effectiveness. This information will then be used to guide future MIP strategies. *($250,000)*

Monitoring malaria epidemiology in areas with insecticide resistance detected among mosquitos
Scaling-up use of long lasting insecticide treated nets (ITNs) has been the principal vector control strategy employed in Tanzania. Currently, pyrethroids are the only class of insecticide vailable for use on ITNs. Increasingly, insecticide resistance, particularly to the pyrethroids, has been detected during routine monitoring. It is unclear to what extent the detected levels of pyrethroid resistance threaten the efficacy of the intervention. Epidemiological surveillance will be conducted over a three year period to measure the level of malaria transmission in four sentinel sites where mosquito resistance to insecticides has been detected as well as one site where resistance has not been detected (control). In addition, hospital data will be collected in order to establish the contribution of malaria to the burden of severe diseases in the respective districts. ($110,800)

Durable Wall Liner (DWL) study
This is a multi-year study funded primarily from TRACTION, with additional support for ITN procurement and IRS for the study area provided by Tanzania. This study aims to assess the protective efficacy of DWL plus ITN and IRS plus ITNs vs. ITNs alone. The baseline cross-sectional survey is planned for July of 2013, at which time the incidence cohort of 6-59 month old children who will be tested for malaria monthly, will be recruited. Distribution of ITNs will occur in October/November of 2013. Insecticide Treated Wall Liner (ITWL) installation and spraying of IRS will begin in January of 2014. Two additional cross-sectional surveys will be conducted in July of 2014 and 2015. In addition to the outcome of malaria, anemia and Lymphatic Filariasis will be tested in during the cross-sectional surveys and a cost-effectiveness analysis will be performed comparing IRS to ITWLs. Tanzania will contribute funds for ITNs and IRS with pyrethroid in this area. ($400,000)

Nationwide Surveys
Secondary Analysis of THMIS and SPA: PMI will contribute funds to conduct a secondary analysis of the 2011/12 THMIS and the upcoming 2013 TSPA. Areas for secondary analysis will include: the relationship between malaria prevalence and anemia; and the characteristics of regions that showed marked reduction in malaria prevalence in 2011/12 THMIS in comparison with those that showed minimal or no reduction in malaria prevalence; and the relationship between malaria prevalence and service availability, readiness, and quality. ($100,000)

Demographic and Health Survey. Provide support for implementation of the 2014-15 DHS, which provides critical outcome and impact data. The DHS will be co-funded with other USG health programs and will include malaria prevalence biomaker. *($300,000)*

6. BEHAVIOR CHANGE COMMUNICATION (BCC)

NMCP//ZMCP/PMI Objectives
Mainland and Zanzibar
The NMCP's and ZMCP's BCC goal is to improve BCC so that a high proportion of the population at risk of malaria will be aware of the appropriate use of malaria prevention and treatment interventions. The NMCP and ZMCP BCC strategic plans aim to advocate for, and communicate positive behaviors for malaria control. The BCC strategic plans serve as guides to coordinate efforts, messages and activities for all malaria implementing partners. The communication strategies address the various levels of health care, namely: central level for policy formulation and resource mobilization; local government level for planning and budgeting for malaria control interventions; service delivery to improve interpersonal communication and compliance to standards; and at community level to improve demand, use, and compliance. The BCC strategies also target the media and pressure groups to improve advocacy for improved resources for malaria control and to communicate policies and services to the community.

Progress during the last 12 months
Early 2012, USAID/Tanzania conducted a mid-term evaluation of the JHU/COMMIT project that showed that when communities are properly mobilized they can take the necessary action to change individual and community behavior.[3] The PMI-funded Community Change Agent (CCA)

---

[3] GH Tech Bridge Project (June 2012) "USAID/Tanzania: COMMIT Project Performance Evaluation"

assessment also showed that people who had some contact with CCAs reported changing their behaviors around net use and case management. For the radio program, parents reported that their children were agents of change in their households and community.

The evaluation recommended that, "A fresh look at the issues related to the elements of desired behaviors, and the circumstance that aid and inhibit the adoption of these behaviors is needed as the basis for the formulation of new policies, systems, activities that can stimulate high levels of the behaviors the MOHSW seek to instill."

The 2011/12 THMIS reported that 92% of women knew a symptom of malaria, and awareness of malaria is universal, over 98%. Eighty three percent of women and 91% of men had heard or seen the *Malaria Haikubaliki* (No More Malaria) slogan used on all malaria BCC materials in Tanzania, and 57% of women and 67% of men had heard or seen a malaria prevention message. The survey also found that women understand that pregnant women are at high risk of malaria (90%), that they could protect their children from malaria (82%), and that it was important to sleep under a net every night (93%).

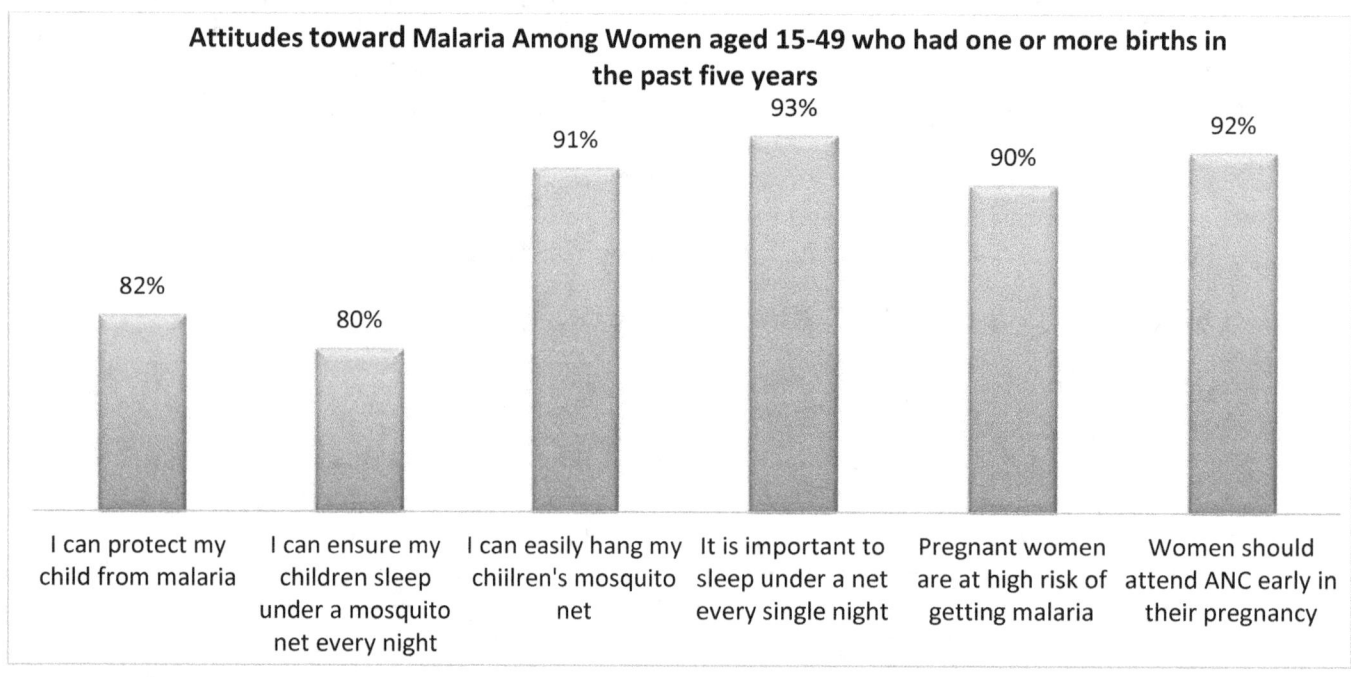

In October 2012, PMI, leveraged USAID PEPFAR and Maternal and Child Health funds to introduce a national integrated safe motherhood (SM) campaign locally known as *Wazazi Nipendeni* (literally translated as "my parents please love me"). The campaign uses SMS technology to send weekly messages to service providers and health workers and pregnant women subscribers receive weekly reminders to go for antenatal care early, test for HIV/AIDS and go for prevention of mother to child transmission (PMTCT+) services, request for the ITN vouchers, request SP for IPTp, and develop an individual birth plan. PMI also supported the SM campaign through radio, TV, and print materials for health clinics. An Omnibus survey conducted in March 2013 in all regions of Mainland showed that exposure to the SM campaign was about 43%. As of November 2012, 139,970 people had registered to receive the pregnant woman reminders text messaging service. The campaign is monitored quarterly through

Omnibus surveys, clinic data, and SMS registration reporting. Additionally, PMI will support the evaluation of the SMC through an exit interview survey with ANC clients and women who delivered during the campaign period. The exit interview will be conducted between August and October 2013.

PMI supported the BCC activities for the pilot school-based net distribution campaign using posters, episodes on children's radio program, discussion guides, games and quizzes, and radio public service announcements. The messaging explained the design of the program, who would get the nets, redistribution of nets, use of and caring and repair of nets.

PMI also continued the support CCA program for community mobilization, and supported technical assistance for developing district malaria plans that could be funded through the Comprehensive Council Health Plans to improve sustainability of malaria BCC efforts.

Challenges, opportunities, and threats
The 2011/12 THMIS showed major gaps in positive behaviors and use of malaria interventions. Although there is universal knowledge about malaria and positive attitudes for malaria prevention, the data shows a net coverage of only 68% for households, 72% for children under five, and 75% for pregnant women. Net use is even lower in Zanzibar at 44% for households, 51% for under-five children, and 36% for pregnant women. The same survey shows high IPTp dropout rate and low testing for malaria. IPTp1 coverage is 60% yet IPTp2 coverage is low at 32%. Of the 20% children under the age of five that had fever on two weeks before the survey, only 77% were seen by a professional health worker, out of whom only 25% had a blood test and only 34% were given an antimalarial drug on the same or next day. Only about 5% of men and women were visited by a health worker or volunteer to talk about malaria in the last six months.

The introduction of SMS technology to communicate malaria safe motherhood messages provides an opportunity to enlarge the scope to include messaging on demanding for malaria testing and compliance to test results. A new IPTp policy adopted by the government will make it easier to communicate IPTp messages and minimize missed opportunities.

The RDT scale up on Mainland provides a platform for a new case management campaign focusing on testing and adhering to test results. The biggest threat is to make BCC interventions relevant and reduce complacency as malaria prevalence goes down. With lower levels of malaria transmission, the community may not see the need to consistently sleep under a net.

Plans and justification
Mainland
BCC efforts will build on the JHU/COMMIT findings and look for more ways to engage communities in the behavior change process. This includes moving communities to collective action where they discuss and identify activities they can undertake to improve malaria prevention outcomes, mobilizing communities and schools through volunteers for net care and repair activities, celebrating communities that have achieved malaria prevention goals, and linking volunteers to health facilities to make impacts on malaria in pregnancy outcomes.

Media activities will be used as a catalyst to initiate community level discussions on various themes such as malaria in pregnancy, case management, and net use. These community gatherings allow a more in-depth discussion on the themes through interaction with the facilitators and the movies shown. This will be followed up with the volunteers for specific community actions.

The mass media will be used to echo and model the community actions being undertaken. Community radio programs will be used to highlight the actions happening locally and celebrating the achievement of success. This "recognition" serves as an incentive for communities to take action around malaria prevention, treatment, and control.

For ITNs, PMI support will prioritize BCC messages in regions with lower than 80% net use for intensified and localized messaging and community mobilization. Where necessary, home visits and hang-up campaigns will educate communities on consistent net use and care and repair. Regions with higher than 80% net use will receive behavior re-enforcement to maintain high coverage. IRS messages will be used to communicate the need to cooperate with spray teams and to prepare districts and communities for scale down/phase out of IRS.
For MIP, BCC messages will focus on improving IPTp2 coverage by advocating for and promoting the new IPTp plus policy. PMI will expand the reach of the electronic SM campaign to more regions. For malaria case management, FY 2014 funding will focus on improving malaria testing and compliance to test results, proper malaria management, and early seeking for malaria treatment. Effort will be made to integrate case management messaging into the electronic SM campaign.

Zanzibar
PMI is supporting Zanzibar to develop a new communication strategy that addresses the current malaria epidemiology and scale of malaria pre-elimination interventions. PMI will support ZMCP to implement sustained and integrated BCC campaign for ITN use, early health seeking and testing, and compliance to test results.

Peace Corps
PMI supports three Peace Corps Volunteers who work very closely with NMCP and other implementing partners to assist with the school net pilot program in Lindi and Mtwara and to focus on school net program awareness creation and behavior change activities. PMI has also expanded the volunteers' scope to support surveillance activities in the Lake Zone region, i.e., training and IRS data collection and analysis. During the past 18 months, Peace Corps has trained 90 volunteers and 64 counterparts on malaria prevention through social behavior change communication messages, field practice, and use of mobile video unit (MVU) and school interventions strategies such as Pata Pata, the children's radio programs. Peace Corps volunteers were also engaged in World Malaria Day events and supported nets distribution and hanging demonstration events at clinics and aided in the distribution of malaria BCC materials.

Proposed activities with FY 2014 funding
Mainland
ITN keep-up strategy. Support to BCC to promote the scale up of the School Net Program or alternative that NMCP decides upon. *($400,000)*

IRS. Mobilize districts and communities, communicating change in IRS strategy, such as moving from blanked to targeted and to focal spraying, and communicating changes in insecticide being used. *($200,000)*

RDT testing and compliance. To advocate for and mobilize service providers and communities for improved testing, compliance to test results, and compliance to malaria diagnostic and treatment guidelines, and seeking treatment within 24 hours of onset of fever. *($800,000)*

Safe Motherhood Campaign. BCC to help scale up the SM campaign ensuring malaria messages are incorporated into the campaign platform and improve service provider interpersonal communication skills. The money will support mass media, print materials, interpersonal communication skills and rural communication initiative. *($600,000)*

Peace Corps Volunteers BCC and Malaria Surveillance
PMI will support three Peace Corps Volunteers to work with the NMCP and PMI implementing partners to assist with BCC activities, including distribution and hanging of nets; organizing malaria awareness and behavior change activities, community talks, theatre, radio spots, house-to-house counseling; and to assist with dissemination of health messages. PMI will also support volunteers to engage in malaria surveillance activities, i.e., to assist in developing training materials and tools for implementation of surveillance activities. They will also assist in systematic collection, analysis and interpretation of data. The malaria volunteers will continue to receive technical support from Peace Corps staff, PMI, NMCP through Regional Malaria Intervention Focal Persons (RMIFP) and other NGOs. ($30,000)

Zanzibar
BCC support for ITN continuous distribution, malaria diagnostic testing, adherence to treatment regimens, education and mobilization for outbreak response; and communicating insecticide rotation and IRS phase out. *($200,000)*

7. HEALTH SYSTEM STRENGTHENING/CAPACITY BUILDING

PMI/NMCP/ZMCP Objectives
Both Mainland and Zanzibar Ministries of Health have prioritized human resources for health, health financing, health management information system, and logistics management as the priorities for health systems strengthening. To improve ownership and management of malaria activities, the NMCP and ZMCP strategic plans prioritize capacity building as a cross cutting intervention for both programs. Using PMI funds for health systems strengthening and capacity building interventions will strengthen the capacity of host-country workforces to ensure an integrated and sustainable approach to malaria prevention and control.

Progress since PMI started in 2006
Since 2006, PMI has supported health systems strengthening initiatives through a number of activities, including information system strengthening for the supply chain, capacity building efforts of the National Bureau of Statistics to conduct major national surveys and finally co-supporting broader strengthening efforts for human resources planning, budgeting, and financial

management by the GOT. PMI has leveraged its resources by co-funding health systems strengthening and capacity building activities related to: human resources for health which addresses workforce planning and management; improving governance and accountability which focuses on strengthening budgeting and management capabilities at the local government authority level, and developing local capacities of NMCP and ZMCP for effective management and coordination of malaria activities.

The African Field Epidemiology Network, the USAID Global Health Bureau, CDC-Atlanta and CDC-Tanzania (with PEPFAR funding) have all worked with PMI and PEFAR since 2007 to develop and strengthen the Tanzania Field Epidemiology and Laboratory Training Program (FELTP). FELTP is a public health training program to enhance competencies in applied epidemiology, implementation, evaluation, and management of disease interventions, surveillance strengthening, epidemic preparedness and response, and leadership skills. The Program is managed by the MOHSW in collaboration with Muhimbili University of Health and Allied Sciences and National Institute of Medical Research.

During the two-year program, FELTP trainees are embedded within the MOHSW where they work daily with the staff of specific disease control programs (e.g., NMCP and ZMCP). Residents have been conducting evaluations of malaria surveillance systems and planned studies on issues related to malaria and malaria diagnostics continuously since program inception. To date, there have been three graduating classes of 29 FELTP students, out of whom, 24 have been returned to government institutions and five are employed in the private sector.

Progress in the last 12 months
PMI support to systems strengthening initiatives has impacted the district level. Specifically, the governance and accountability activities influenced the Local Government Authorities (LGA) to integrate malaria in the Comprehensive Council Health Plans (CCHPs) and PMI funds enabled the health facility planning teams to use local data to identify community needs and priority areas, including malaria. These issues were then incorporated into district CCHPs and budgets; 70% of targeted health facilities are now using their own cost-sharing funds to contribute to procuring malaria medicines and supplies. Having benefited from technical support to strengthen internal controls and to use key financial management and planning tools (Epicor and PlanRep3), PMI-supported councils are now more efficient and rationalize the use of resources, including for malaria control and procurement. Using the new financial management software (Epicor), councils are not allowed to shift funds so funds planned for malaria must be used for malaria related activities.

Investment in HRH planning, recruitment, and retention has resulted in improved LGA ability to recruit critical staff needed for malaria case management. PMI supported human resources for health activities include the development and use of a comprehensive HR information system at the district level, leading to the informed deployment of health workers to communities that are hardest to reach. PMI investment in the development of HR information systems has allowed the country to better track its staffing progress such as vacancy rates, deployment and geographical coverage. Findings from this information have found that in the Lake Zone alone, our investment in workforce planning has resulted in a drop in vacancy rates of health care workers from 40% to

36%. This information system is now accessible in every district council in the country, including Zanzibar.

FELTP students made presentations at several conferences on topics, such as "Effect of intermittent preventive treatment for preventing malaria infection during pregnancy using sulphadoxine-pyrimethamine on birth weight in Lindi Region, 2009" and "Assessment of availability and factors that influence the prescription of antimalarials, Iringa Region, 2011." All trainees participate in outbreak investigations in Tanzania, thereby developing their skills for future malaria outbreak investigations, in 2012 residents participated in 11 outbreak investigations such as cholera outbreak in Mtwara January 2012, measles outbreak in Morogoro, and Ebola outbreak in Kibaale District in Uganda. The CDC resident advisor has assisted with mentoring these trainees and participates in classroom teaching (surveillance, study design, outbreak investigation, data analysis). The fourth cohort of 12 trainees graduated in December 2013.

Challenges, opportunities, and threats
The main challenges are health work staffing shortages at all levels (particularly in rural areas and among mid-level cadres), pharmaceutical stockouts, and insufficient financing for health care. These issues are further compounded by poor communication between the levels of the health system, inadequate mechanisms for accountability, weak leadership and management skills, and imbalances between well-resourced, vertical programs and the rest of the health care system (for example, HIV and malaria programs account for 46% of all health expenditures in Tanzania).

Despite the challenges, there are a number of reform opportunities on the horizon. These include the high-level development of a national health care financing strategy (which is likely to include the plans for the establishment of a 'health trust' fund), the selection of the health sector by the President to conduct accelerated reform to produce results ("Big Results Now" initiative), increasing focus on value for money strategies (such as Pay for Performance), development of key national human resources for health strategies and staffing norms, increased support for formalization of a community worker cadre, and a national assessment to guide supply chain reforms.

Plans and Justification
The Tanzania Mission intends to support health systems strengthening in an integrated fashion that brings together the key WHO Health System Building Blocks of 'finance,' 'human resources,' and 'governance' at the national and the local level. This approach reflects the current global thinking of the need to link efforts between the various building blocks to maximize impact. PMI funds will capitalize on these opportunities and work to address health systems issues affecting malaria outcomes. PMI-funded health systems strengthening activities will address the underlying systems challenges impinging upon progress towards national malaria goals.

PMI funds will be used to address the underlying malaria challenges in a holistic way, addressing health care financing, governance and staffing issues at the national and at the LGA level. Specific activities include strengthening domestic investment in health including malaria, improving staffing recruitment and retention, and strengthening GOT planning and budgeting such that they are based on burden of disease.

At the national level, HSS effort will be made to ensure the inclusion of current and anticipated costs for malaria in the roll-out of the country's first national health care financing strategy. This strategy, currently in development, explores how to generate domestic resources both public and private, through innovative approaches such as tapping into natural gas revenue for a health trust fund. The goal is increased domestic resources for health. HSS efforts in this regard will directly ensure the financial sustainability of the malaria program in Tanzania. The Mission is planning to conduct specific HSS baseline and follow-up evaluations to measure the impact. PMI/Tanzania and USAID are developing indicators to track progress on an annual basis.

At the LGA level, HSS effort will target LGA ability to better recruit and retain staff and to use their own generated resources such as money from cost-sharing, private sector partnerships, or performance based financing, to strengthen service delivery for health care. This is inclusive of the needs for case management and community participation in malaria (case management, IRS etc.). The goal is to decrease vacancy rates, particularly for those cadres involved in malaria case management, and increase the LGA budget allocation as needed for malaria. This will be informed by a specific HSS evaluation to measure impact. PMI/Tanzania and USAID are developing indicators to track progress on an annual basis.

PMI support is largely for technical assistance and not intended for direct granting to LGAs. This will be assessed routinely and in the event direct funding for LGAS is needed, PMI will find an appropriate channel to do this.

Proposed Activities with FY 2014 Funding

Mainland
Support to FELTP Program. PMI will continue support to the FELTP program and contribute to the advanced training of Tanzanian epidemiologists for a 12-month period. The trainees will receive assistance from Resident Advisors and participate in malaria field assignments and investigations throughout Mainland and Zanzibar. PMI will continue to track the placement of FELTP graduates into post-training MOHSW assignments that directly influence malaria control policies and practices. *($150,000)*

Support to National Health Systems Strengthening. PMI funds will be used to support the national health systems strengthening efforts to inform the roll out of the national health care financing strategy as well as to establish routine monitoring of financial costs, needs, and gaps relating to malaria interventions. To demonstrate 'value for money' and bolster the case for Ministry of Finance investment in health, PMI funds will be used to provide technical assistance and incorporation of malaria considerations into innovative financing initiatives, such as the national "Pay for Performance" program. Funding will also be used to develop and operationalize human resources for health strategies for recruitment and particularly for retention of staff, including those pivotal to the delivery of malaria services. For example, to strengthen health promotion, PMI will support the GOT to analyze workforce considerations and recommendations for formalizing a community health worker cadre. *($450,000)*

Local Government Authority HSS. FY 2014 funds will support districts to strengthen their use of evidence-based processes for budgeting, planning, coordination and management duties of malaria activities. Technical support will be given to LGAs to explore domestic financing opportunities for malaria like cost sharing and public-private partnerships. PMI FY 2014 funds also continue previous efforts to strengthen LGA financial accountability mechanisms, their internal controls, and their ability to rationalize resources effectively for health care, including malaria interventions. Additionally, FY 2014 funds will support LGAs to determine workforce needs, strengthen their management practices, and implement effective retention strategies for health care workers in rural settings, particularly those trained by PMI. *($400,000)*

Zanzibar
ZMCP capacity building. PMI funds will provide in-service continuous education to ZMCP staff for surveillance and entomological monitoring, data management, malaria diagnostics quality assurance and quality control, and PCR techniques. *($69,000)*

8. STAFFING AND ADMINISTRATION

Background
Two expatriate health professionals (Resident Advisors) oversee PMI in Tanzania: one representing CDC and the other USAID. Two full-time Foreign Service Nationals (FSNs) Program Management Specialists were hired to support the PMI team, one representing CDC and the other USAID. In addition, PMI is providing partial support to two full-time USAID FSNs: a Monitoring & Evaluation (M&E) Officer and Acquisition & Assistance (A&A) Specialist. The M&E Officer manages the PMI M&E agenda, PMI program monitoring plan, web-based reporting, data quality audits, and assists implementing partners to develop monitoring and evaluation plans. The A&A Specialist attends to the procurement actions for PMI and ensures compliance to USAID contractual and financial regulations. Four other U.S. PSC and FSNs are managing PMI funded activities that are integrated in other heath and HIV programs but their salaries are covered by non-PMI funds. A U.S. Personal Services Contractor (USPSC) assists the PMI team (part time) as Agreement Officer Representative or Activity Manager and is partially supported by PMI funding. One U.S. Direct Hire, two U.S.PSC, and one FSN are Agreement Officer Representatives or Activity Managers for PMI funded activities that are integrated in other heath and HIV programs but their salaries are covered by non-PMI funds.

All PMI staff members are part of a single interagency team led by the USAID Mission Director or his/her designee in country. The PMI team shares responsibility for development and implementation of PMI strategies and work plans, coordination with national authorities, managing collaborating agencies and supervising day-to-day activities. Candidates for resident advisor positions (whether initial hires or replacements) will be evaluated and/or interviewed jointly by USAID and CDC, and both agencies will be involved in hiring decisions, with the final decision made by the individual agency.

The PMI professional staff work together to oversee all technical and administrative aspects of the PMI portfolio, including finalizing details of the project design, implementing malaria prevention and treatment activities, monitoring and evaluation of outcomes and impact, reporting of results, and providing guidance to PMI partners.

The PMI lead in country is the USAID Mission Director. The two PMI resident advisors, one from USAID and one from CDC, report to the Senior USAID Health Officer for day-to-day leadership, and work together as a part of a single interagency team. The technical expertise housed in Atlanta and Washington guides PMI programmatic efforts and thus overall technical guidance for both RAs falls to the PMI staff in Atlanta and Washington. Since CDC resident advisors are CDC employees (CDC USDD—38), responsibility for completing official performance reviews lies with the CDC Country Director who is expected to rely upon input from PMI staff across the two agencies that work closely day in and day out with the CDC RA and, thus, best positioned to comment on the RA's performance.

The two PMI resident advisors are based within the USAID health office and are expected to spend approximately half their time sitting with and providing technical assistance to the national malaria control programs and partners.

Locally-hired staff to support PMI activities either in Ministries or in USAID will be approved by the USAID Mission Director. Because of the need to adhere to specific country policies and USAID accounting regulations, any transfer of PMI funds directly to Ministries or host governments will need to be approved by the USAID Mission Director and Controller, in addition to the PMI Coordinator.

All technical activities are undertaken in close coordination with the Ministry of Health NMCP and ZMCP and other national and international partners, including WHO, UNICEF, the Global Fund, World Bank, DFID, the Embassy of the Kingdom of the Netherlands, the Swiss Agency for Development and Cooperation, and the private sector.

Proposed Activities with FY 2014 Funding

PMI will support salaries and travel costs of the two PMI Resident Advisors, the two FSN PMI Project Management Specialists, the M&E Officer, the A&A Specialist, and half the salary of a USPSC managing some of the PMI portfolio. Total management and administrative costs, excluding the salary and benefits of the USAID and CDC PMI Resident advisors and locally employed PMI staff is approximately 2% of the total budget. Total ($2,490,000)

TABLE 1 - BUDGET BREAKDOWN BY PARTNER			
President's Malaria Initiative - Mainland Tanzania and Zanzibar Year 9 (FY14) Budget Breakdown by Implementing Partner			
Partner Organization	Geographic Area	Activity	Budget
CDC	National	CDC staffing and administration	$660,000
	National	TDYs	$84,700
	National	FELTP	$150,000
	Zanzibar	Reagant Procurement	$10,000
ICF MACRO	National	Secondary Analysis of THMIS and TSPA	$100,000
	National	Tanzania "DHS"	$300,000
JHU - TCCP	Mainland	Behavior Change Communication	2,000,000
NMCP	Mainland	mRDT Strengthening including QA/QC System	$100,000
	Mainland	iCCM	$100,000
	Mainland	Roll-out of new NGDT and IPTp	$1,000,000
	Mainland	Malaria Program Review	$25,000
	Mainland	Integrated Supportive Supervision	$500,000
Peace Corps	National	BCC across all intervention areas by Peace Corps Volunteers	$30,000
RTI	Mainland	Indoor Residual Spraying	$14,823,000
	Zanzibar	Indoor Residual Spraying	$500,000
	Zanzibar	MEEDS	$300,000
	Mainland	Routine Malaria Surveillance System	$500,000
	Mainland	Durable Wall Lining Study IRS	$200,000
	Zanzibar	PCR Establishment, training and procurement	$94,000
	Mainland	Entomologic Monitoring	$650,000
TBD	Mainland	Health Systems Strenghthening district level	$450,000
	Mainland	Health System Strengthening National Level	$400,000
	Mainland	Malaria in Pregnancy	$2,500,000
	Mainland	SP Resistance Monitoring related to IPTp	$250,000
	Mainland	ITN Keep up Program	$8,243,500
	Mainland	mRDT Strengthening including QA/QC System	$1,900,000
	Mainland	Routine Therapeutic Drug Efficacy Monitoring	$250,000
	Mainland	End of project Evaluation for URC and JHU-TCCP	$125,000
	National	Mission-wide M & E Contracts	$390,000
	Mainland	Monitoring malaria epidemiology in	$110,800

		areas where mosquitoes have developed resistance to insecticides	
URC	Mainland	Service Delivery Strengthening	$750,000
USAID	National	USAID Staffing and administration	$1,830,000
JSI| DELIVER	Zanzibar	RDT Procurement	$400,000
	Mainland	RDT Procurement for UNHCR	$50,000
	Mainland	RDT Procurement	$1,000,000
	Mainland	ACT Procurement	$2,000,000
	Mainland	ACT Procurement for UNHCR	$50,000
	Zanzibar	Repackaging of ACTs	$100,000
	Zanzibar	Primaquine Procurement	$1,000
	Mainland	ITNs for Durable Wall Lining study	$200,000
	Mainland	Malaria Commodity Logistics	$750,000
	Zanzibar	Malaria Commodity Logistics	$250,000
ZMCP	Zanzibar	Behavior Change Communication	$200,000
	Zanzibar	RDT and Microscopy QA/QC	$104,000
	Zanzibar	Updating case management guideline including treatment of primaquine	$50,000
	Zanzibar	Integrated Supportive Supervison	$40,000
	Zanzibar	Capacity Building of ZMCP Staff	$69,000
	Zanzibar	MEEDS reporting and outbreak response	$250,000
	Zanzibar	Entomological Monitoring	$160,000
GRAND TOTAL			**$45,000,000**

Table 2
President's Malaria Initiative – *Tanzania Mainland and Zanzibar*
Planned Obligations for FY14 ($45,000,000)

Proposed Activity	Mechanism	Geographic Area	PMI Proposed FY 2014	Brief Description of Activity
PREVENTIVE ACTIVITIES				
Insecticide Treated Nets				
Keep-up Program	*TBD*	Mainland	8,243,500	Procure and distribute 1.4 million ITNs through school-based program, mass distribution, or another approach to be determined by NMCP
Keep-up Program	*TBD*	Zanzibar	0	PMI will use FY 2013 funds to help support distribution costs of Global Fund procured ITNs
Indoor Residual Spraying				
Mainland IRS	*RTI*	Mainland	14,823,000	Targeted spraying in Mwanza and Mara with one round using Acteric CS and exapnsion of IRS to Geita and Kigoma regions using Vectron (one round).
Zanzibar IRS	*RTI*	Zanzibar	500,000	Focal spraying of malaria hot spots in up to 25,000 structures
Malaria in Pregnancy				
Health systems strengthening for IPTp 2 implementation and Supportive Supervision by DHMTs	*TBD*	Mainland	2,500,000	Comprehensive support to proposed new IPTp policy adoption and implementation, including development/dissemination of training materials, supervision, supply chain management for SP, and Safe Motherhood Campaign
Technical assistance-MIP	*CDC*	Mainland	12,100	CDC staff will provide technical support to implementation of new WHO IPT guidelines and strategies to improve IPT
SUBTOTAL: Preventive Activities			**26,078,600**	

CASE MANAGEMENT ACTIVITIES

Diagnostics

Activity		Location	Amount	Description
mRDT strengthening including QA/QC system	TBD	Mainland	1,900,000	Scale up of national QA/QC system focused on RDTs
	NMCP	Mainland	100,000	Direct support to NMCP to allow supervision of RDT QA/QC system
mRDT and Microscopy	ZMCP	Nationwide	104,000	Establishment of slide bank, implementation of QA/QC system
	JSI	Zanzibar	400,000	Procure about 500,000RDTs for health facilities, active case detection, and outbreak use
RDT Procurement	JSI	Mainland	50,000	RDT procurement for UNCHR refugee camps
	JSI	Mainland	1,000,000	Funding for about 1.2million RDTs if delays occur with other donor funding
Technical Assistance-Case Management	CDC	Nationwide	12,100	Technical assistance for the implementation of quality assurance and quality control program

Malaria Treatment

Activity		Location	Amount	Description
Management of Febrile Illness	URC	Mainland	750,000	Support to Tibu Homa febrile case management project in Lake Zone
ACT Procurement	JSI	Mainland	2,000,000	Funding for about 2 million AL treatments if delays occur in other donor support
	JSI	Mainland	50,000	ACT procurement for UNHCR camp
Procurement of Primaquine	JSI	Zanzibar	1,000	Procure primaquine for new ZMCP malaria treatment policy
Repackaging of ACTs	JSI	Zanzibar	100,000	Repackaging of ACTs to minimize waste
iCCM	NMCP	Mainland	100,000	Support to NCMP to oversee case management of malaria in children under five
Malaria Commodity Logistics	JSI	Mainland	750,000	Strengthen quantification, distribution, storage, inventory management of malaria commodities
	JSI	Zanzibar		Strengthen quantification, distribution, storage,

MONITORING and EVALUATION

Activity	Implementer	Location	Cost	Description
			250,000	inventory management of malaria commodities
Roll-out of new National Guideline Diagnosis and Treatment and IPTp	*NMCP/ZTCs*	Mainland	1,000,000	Support to training and supervision related to new malaria diagnosis and treatment guidelines and new IPTp guidelines
Updating case mgmt guideline including treatment with primaquine	*ZMCP*	Zanzibar	50,000	Support to training and supervision related to new malaria diagnosis and treatment guidelines and new IPTp guidelines
Routine Therapeutic Drug Efficacy Monitoring	*TBD*	Mainland	250,000	Routine therapeutic monitoring of parasite clearance following AL treatment in hospitalized patients at four to five sites
SUBTOTAL: Case Management			**8,867,100**	

MONITORING and EVALUATION

Epidemic Surveillance and Response

Activity	Implementer	Location	Cost	Description
Routine Malaria Surveillance System	*RTI*	Mainland	500,000	Support to paper-based malaria surveillance in Lake Zone until electronic IDSR reporting system becomes operational
MEEDS reporting and outbreak response	*RTI*	Zanzibar	300,000	Technical assistance and support for day-to-day operation of MEEDS system
Re. & Pro Active Case Detection	*ZMCP*	Zanzibar	250,000	Direct support to ZMCP to oversee/supervise MEEDS network
SUBTOTAL: Epidemic Surveillance			**1,050,000**	

Monitoring and Evaluation Support

Activity	Implementer	Location	Cost	Description
Integrated Supportive Supervision and Coordination including bi-annual meeting with CHMT/DHMT/RHMT	*NMCP*	Mainland	500,000	Strengthen NMCP M&E Unit to collect, analyze, and disseminate data on malaria activities
	ZMCP	Zanzibar	40,000	Support integrated health facility visits for supervision of laboratory and surveillance activities
Malaria Program Review	*NMCP*	Mainland		PMI's contribution to the NMCP malaria program

Activity	Organization	Location	Amount	Description
			25,000	review
Mission-wide M & E Contract including mid-term and end of project evaluation	*Mission wide M&E Contractor*	Nationwide	390,000	PMI contribution to USAID M&E contract
URC end of project evaluation	*Mission wide M&E Contractor*	Mainland	100,000	PMI contribution to end of project evaluation for integrated febrile case management project in Lake Zone
JHU-TCCP end of project evaluation	*Mission wide M&E Contractor*	Mainland	25,000	PMI contribution to end of project evaluation for Johns Hopkins University BCC bilateral project
Technical Assistance-M&E	*CDC*	Nationwide	24,200	CDC staff will conduct two TA visits to assist with changes in M&E programming
Entomological Monitoring				
Entomological and insecticide resistance Monitoring including establishment & procurement of PCR	*RTI - NIMR*	Mainland	650,000	Support 26 entomologic sentinel surveillance sites
	RTI	Zanzibar	94,000	Support entomologic sentinel surveillance sites on islands of Pemba and Unjuga
	ZMCP	Zanzibar	160,000	Support entomologic sentinel surveillance sites on islands of Pemba and Unjuga
Reagent Procurement	*CDC*	Zanzibar	10,000	Funding for purchase of entomologic supplies not readily available in Tanzania
Technical Assistance- Entomological Monitoring	*CDC*	Nationwide	24,200	Two TA visits to provide technical assistance to NIMR Mwanza to achieve the necessary routine entomologic monitoring of post spray activities and to monitor the entomology effects of the U5CC and the UCC in non-IRS area. In Zanzibar CDC will provide technical assistance to increase ELISA capability to include blood meal analysis for vector biting preferences and essays for mosquitoes. This activity includes technical support for entomological supplies because the reagents have been difficult to obtain locally.

Name	Partner	Location	Amount	Description
Technical Assistance-PCR	_CDC_	Zanzibar	12,100	CDC staff will conduct one TA visit to assist with capacity building for PCR.
Operational Research				
SP Resistance Monitoring related to IPTp	_TBD_	Mainland	250,000	Monitor SP resistance and effectiveness because of risks associated with SP use of IPTp in area with high-level resistance
Monitoring malaria epidemiology in areas where mosquitoes have developed resistance to insecticides	_TBD_	Mainland	110,800	Evaluation of impact of insecticide resistance on effect of ITNS on malaria epidemiology
Durable Wall Lining Study	_JSI_	Mainland	200,000	Procurement of ITNs for households and money to cover expense of IRS for study. It is expected the wall linings will be provided free of charge.
	RTI	Mainland	200,000	
Nationwide Surveys				
Secondary analysis of THMIS &TSPA	_ICF Macro_	Nationwide	100,000	Secondary analysis of the 2011/12 THMIS& 2013 TSPA. Areas for secondary analysis will include: the relationship between malaria prevalence and anemia;
DHS 2015	_ICF Macro_	Nationwide	300,000	PMI contribution to 2015 DHS implementation
SUBTOTAL: MONITORING AND EVALUATION			**_3,215,300_**	
BCC				
BCC Across all interventions	_JHU-TCCP_	Mainland	2,000,000	BCC interventions for all malaria interventions including information related to new IPTp policies for both the Mainland and Zanzibar.
	ZMCP	Zanzibar	200,000	
Peace Corps Volunteer BCC	_Peace Corps Tanzania_	Mainland	30,000	Support for three Peace Corps Volunteers
SUBTOTAL: BCC			**_2,230,000_**	
HEALTH SYSTEMS STRENGTHENING AND CAPACITY BUILDING				
Field Epidemiology & Laboratory Training Program				

Activity	Implementer	Location	Amount	Description
Continue Support to FELTP	*CDC*	Nationwide	150,000	Support to FELTP trainees with focus on malaria
Health System Strengthening				
Strengthening of National Health Systems	*TBD*	Mainland	450,000	Support the national health systems strengthening efforts to inform the roll out of the national health care financing strategy as well as to establish routine monitoring of financial costs, needs, and gaps relating to malaria interventions.
Local Government Authority HSS	*TBD*	Mainland	400,000	Support districts to strengthen their use of evidence-based processes for budgeting, planning, coordination and management duties of malaria activities. Technical support will be given to LGAs to explore domestic financing opportunities for malaria like cost sharing and public-private partnerships.
ZMCP Staff Capacity Building	*ZMCP*	Zanzibar	69,000	In-country or regional training and capacity building of ZMCP staff
SUBTOTAL: HSS & Capacity Building			**1,069,000**	
MANAGEMENT AND ADMINISTRATION				
USAID staff	*USAID*	Nationwide	1,830,000	Support for salaries, benefits and administrative costs
CDC staff	*USAID*	Nationwide	660,000	
SUBTOTAL: Management and Administration			**2,490,000**	
GRAND TOTAL			**45,000,000**	

www.ingramcontent.com/pod-product-compliance
Lightning Source LLC
Chambersburg PA
CBHW080519290526
45790CB00006B/2239

*9 7 8 1 5 0 3 0 5 2 7 0 3 *